The Ministry of the Word

By G. CAMPBELL MORGAN

EXPOSITORY

The Teaching of Christ. Cloth . . .

The Crises of the Christ. *Popular Edition* .

The Study and Teaching of the English Bible.
Cloth . . . .

The Missionary Manifesto. Being a Study of the
Great Commission . . . . . .

The Analyzed Bible. *Introductory Volumes.* Vols.
I, II, III. Each . . . . . .
Analytical Volumes. Vol. IV, The Gospel Ac-
cording to John. Vol. V, The Book of Job. Vol.
VI, Romans. Vol. VII, VIII, The Prophecy of
Isaiah, I and II. IX, Genesis. X, The Gospel of
Matthew. Each . . . . . .

Living Messages of the Books of the Bible.
Now Complete in Two Volumes. 12mo, cloth, each,
Vol. I, O. T.—Genesis to Malachi. Vol. II, N. T.
—Matthew to Revelation.

The Parables of the Kingdom. Expositions of
Matt. XIII. . . . .

The Spirit of God. Cloth . . . .

A First Century Message to Twentieth Century Christians . . . . . .

God's Methods With Man. In Time—Past, Present and Future. With Colored Chart . . .

Wherein Have We Robbed God ? . . .

God's Perfect Will . . . . . .

The Ten Commandments . . . . .

The Hidden Years at Nazareth . . . .

DEVOTIONAL

Sunrise. " Behold, He Cometh !" Cloth . .

The Bible and the Cross. Cloth . . . .

Christian Principles. Cloth . . . . .

Mountains and Valleys in the Ministry of Jesus.
Boards . . . .

The Practice of Prayer. Cloth . . . .

The Simple Things of the Christian Life. Cloth,

The True Estimate of Life and How to Live.
Cloth . . . .

The Christ of To-Day. What ? Whence ? Whither ?
Cloth . . . .

The Life of the Christian. Cloth . . . .

Evangelism. Cloth . . . . . .

Life Problems . . . .

Discipleship. Cloth . . . . . .

" All Things New." A Message to New Converts.
Paper . . . .

Christ and the Bible. Paper . . . .

*The James Sprunt Lectures delivered at
Union Theological Seminary in Virginia*

The Ministry of the Word

By

G. CAMPBELL MORGAN, D.D.

NEW YORK   CHICAGO

Fleming H. Revell Company

LONDON   AND   EDINBURGH

New York: 158 Fifth Avenue
Chicago: 17 North Wabash Ave.
London: 21 Paternoster Square
Edinburgh: 75 Princes Street

THE WORD OF GOD

MY LORD AND SAVIOUR

Oft when the WORD is on me to deliver,
   Lifts the illusion and the truth lies bare,
Desert or throng, the city or the river,
   Melts in a lucid Paradise of air,—
Only like souls I see the folk thereunder,
   Bound who should conquer, slaves who
      should be kings,—
Hearing their one hope with an empty wonder,
   Sadly contented in a show of things ;—
Then with a rush the intolerable craving
   Shivers throughout me like a trumpet-call,—
Oh to save these ! to perish for their saving,
   Die for their life, be offered for them all !

Contents

PROLOGUE 9

> The title, "The Ministry of the Word."
> The Setting of the Phrase.

I
The Fundamental Conceptions

A. THE MINISTRY 19
B. THE WORD 34

II
The Primitive Ideal

A. THE WORD AS THE TRUTH OF THE APOSTLE 53
B. THE WORD AS THE BURDEN OF THE PROPHET 72
C. THE WORD AS THE GOSPEL OF THE EVAN-
GELIST 92
D. THE WORD AS THE WISDOM OF THE PASTOR
AND TEACHER 112

III
The Modern Application

A. THE CHANGED CONDITIONS . . . 135
B. THE UNCHANGED OBLIGATION . . . 156
C. THE PREPARATION OF THE MINISTRY . . 176
D. THE EXERCISE OF THE VOCATION . . 198

EPILOGUE 215

> The First Responsibility.
> "Prayer."

Prologue

THE phrase which constitutes the general title of these Lectures has been deliberately selected, as giving a Biblical indication of the theme I propose to discuss. It occurs in a very familiar passage in the Book of the Acts of the Apostles. An appreciation of the historic background of that passage, and an understanding of the particular story contained therein, will help us to find our true atmosphere, and so start us on the right lines of our consideration.

The historic background is that of the initiation of the new Age of the Spirit. It has all the freshness and fascination of dawn. It is certainly true that no pages of the Biblical literature are more perennially interesting. We have all read them again and again from childhood, and yet whenever we come back to them, they make the same arresting and inspiring appeal to mind and heart and will. We seem, as we read, to feel the breath of the winds of God, and to burn with the enthusiasm, which created the wonder of the men of Jerusalem, as they observed its flaming forth, in the band of Christian disciples. By the baptism of the Holy Spirit these men and women, who had hitherto been devoted followers of Jesus of Nazareth, were brought into mystic but mighty relationship with Him as the victorious and ascended Lord; and were thus perfectly equipped for witness bearing. Through this witness, the number of believers was rapidly increased. Day by day there were added to the Lord, and so to the glad company, those who received the Holy Spirit. These realized their communion with each other, through their common fellowship with their Lord.

The Day which had thus dawned was a Day of remarkable power, of which there were abundant signs. The healing of the man at the Beautiful Gate of the Temple, as the members of the Jewish council admitted, was a "notable miracle"; and so impressed with this fact were the members of that council, that much as they desired to put an end to the Christian propaganda, they dared not, then, take any further steps against the Apostles; but after threatening them, they permitted them to go back to their own company.

The Day, moreover, was one of a strange and awe-inspiring purity. Within the new fellowship hypocrisy and untruth could not exist, as the swift judgment which fell upon Ananias and Sapphira proved. The effect of this was felt within the Church and beyond it; so that, to use the suggestive phrase of the historian, no man durst *join himself* to them. New members were added by the Lord, and by Him alone.

As the movement grew, hostility became more daring. The Apostles were next imprisoned, but they were supernaturally liberated, and fear fell afresh upon their enemies. Still resisting the power of the Spirit, the rulers beat the Apostles, and then were confronted by the astonishing spectacle of men who rejoiced "that they were counted worthy to suffer dishonour for the Name." Such were these wonderful days. Within the fellowship, "the Twelve" were exercising a ministry of teaching and guidance on behalf of the whole multitude of those who, believing, were being added to the Lord.

The paragraph in which the phrase occurs opens with the words, "In these days"; and reveals their special characteristics in the statement, "the number of the disciples was multiplying." It then records the incident of the difficulty which arose in the distribution of the common funds. This difficulty resulted from the persistence of an old trouble within the Christian atmosphere, that of the mutual suspicion and unfriendliness of the Hellenists and the Hebrews. The former complained, in all probability not without reason, that the Hebrews within the community neglected the Hellenist widows. The dispute itself has no interest for us now, but the way in which it was dealt with leads us to our theme, and throws considerable initial light thereupon.

When the murmuring occurred, the Apostles "called the multitude of the disciples" together. In other words, the difficulty was dealt with by the whole Church in solemn assembly, under the guidance of the Apostles. There was no panic, no dissension. The matter was speedily and smoothly adjusted. In the midst of His people was the Lord Himself, according to His covenant; and He, by the Holy Spirit, made known His will. The action thus taken was a very remarkable one in many ways, but they are not immediately relevant to our theme. One matter, however, is of importance.

This was made the occasion for a necessary and vital division of responsibility in the interest of the life and service of the Church. From henceforth there were to be within her borders two orders in the one ministry; the one having to do with the serving of tables, and the other with the service of the Word. It is in this connection that our phrase occurs. Having charged the Church to elect " men of good report full of the Spirit and of wisdom," for the business of serving tables, the Apostles said; " We will continue steadfastly in prayer, and in *the ministry of the Word.*"

That phrase is one of abiding importance in its revelation of the true nature and method of one aspect of Christian Ministry; that aspect which demands the devotion of the whole time and energy of those called upon to exercise it, and which cannot be perfectly exercised by those whose time and energy are taken up with other matters, however right and proper such matters may be in themselves. Within the phrase itself are contained words which suggest the fundamental conceptions. To these we shall give careful attention before proceeding to deal with the primitive ideal, or attempting to make any modern application. In proportion as we accurately apprehend the significance of the terms " the Ministry " and " the Word," we shall be prepared for a consideration of the whole subject of "the Ministry of the Word," and the privilege and responsibility of those called thereto.

Thus it will be realized that in these lectures I am desirous of considering the subject of the Christian Ministry solely from the standpoint of New Testament ideals. It is, however, inevitable that there should enter into the consideration the element of personal experience and colouring. In the work of preparation I have attempted to avoid that, so far as possible. Necessarily it could not be wholly absent from my own thinking, nor therefore will it be absent from the minds of my hearers. My apology then for the measure in which these personal elements obtain in my outlook must be that of the experience which has created them, and I may be pardoned for referring to them in a few sentences.

My father was a Bible preacher and teacher of no mean order. He was a man of one book, in a sense in which his son never has been. He lived to the four score years, and during that period never read a work of fiction. He had no knowledge of general literature. He did know his Bible. Under his influence and guidance I began to preach, delivering my first public address when a boy of thirteen years of age. From then until now, a period of over forty years, I have continued to preach, except for two years, when, through partial eclipse of faith, I had to face the spectres of the mind.

During the earlier part of the time I was being trained for the work of teaching, and doing that work. Throughout that time I was preaching on Sundays, and conducting evangelistic missions during holidays.

In the year 1886 I gave up my work as a teacher, and devoted myself wholly to evangelistic work. During the later period, that is for the past three and thirty years, I have continued to preach. My work has never been Apostolic, as I understand that phase of ministry, and as I shall presently attempt to explain it. It has been upon occasion Prophetic, constantly Evangelistic, and principally Pastoral and Teaching.

These then are the facts concerning the experiences which must affect my thinking. I have mentioned them now to dismiss them, having recognized them. I trust they will be as little obvious as possible, and that our consideration may be wholly conditioned within Biblical light.

I

The Fundamental Conceptions

A

THE MINISTRY

WITHIN the phrase the "Ministry of
the Word," there is included the
whole conception of the work of
preaching as distinguished from that of serving tables. It should at once be recognized
that this is a distinction which must be made in
practice as well as in theory; but it is equally
important that the distinction should be made
intelligently, that is with scriptural warrant,
rather than on the basis of prejudice or custom.
It must be made in the interest of the work of
preaching, not in that of the preachers. To say
that, is simply to interpret at once the meaning
of the Twelve when they took the action which
set them apart from their brethren. They were
not actuated by any desire to create an order of
superiority for themselves, but wholly by a
passion for the complete success of the particular work to which they were appointed. The

work of serving tables is equally sacred. This is evident from the apostolic description of the character and qualifications of the men who were to be appointed to that work. They were to be men " of good report, full of the Spirit and of wisdom." The two orders of the ministry were not intended to be conceived of as higher and lower. They were equally important and complementary. The work of each was dependent for complete success upon that of the other. Deacons might also be preachers, as we soon discover in the case of Philip the Evangelist. The probability is that in such a case the work of the Diaconate was given up. The story of Philip would lead us to that conclusion. But even if so, it was not because the work of serving tables was not most sacred, but because no man could perfectly fulfil the work of the service of the Word, while occupied in the doing of the other. All this will be even more clearly seen as we go forward with our study.

Our first business must be that of attempting to get these fundamental conceptions clearly before us, for in proportion as we do so, we shall be the better prepared for the fuller considerations and applications which we propose.

The two conceptions are suggested by the terms " The Ministry," and " The Word." The second of these reveals the central and supreme matter; while the first indicates the method by which the work is to be accomplished. We shall devote a Lecture to each. The first, that of the revelation of method suggested by the term " The Ministry," is our subject now.

In order to an understanding of the fundamental conception suggested by the term The Ministry, we will first examine the place which the term occupies in our paragraph, and then glance on to the development of the thought, as it is found in one outstanding passage in the apostolic writings.

Taking the Revised Version, we find three words which we will note; in verse one, *ministration;* in verse two, *serve;* and in verse four, *ministry.* It will be granted at once that these three words represent the same idea. In the Greek New Testament this is even more apparent, where the words respectively are *diakŏnia, diakŏnein,* and *diakŏnia,* the first and the last being identical. The special word of our term then is the word *diakŏnia,* translated *ministration* in verse one, and *ministry* in verse four. What then, quite apart from any interpretation resulting from our habit and custom in the use of the word, is the first and simplest idea that it suggests?

Unquestionably the idea is that of the work of a servant, the carrying out of responsibility under command. The Greek word is derived from the word *diakŏnŏs*, which simply means an attendant, a waiter; which in turn comes from an obsolete verb, *diakō*, to run on errands. The simple thought then is that of service in the most elemental sense, that of having work appointed, and that of doing that work under mastery. Let us carefully observe that this idea is never properly eliminated, nor changed in any subsequent use of the word. That is the thought in the first verse. The daily *ministration* was that of the actual giving out, from the common fund, of the appointed portions to the needy members of the community. Obviously it is equally the thought of the word *serve* in the second verse. When the Apostles declared that it was not meet that they should serve tables, they simply meant that the urgency of the work to which they were specifically appointed was such, that neither their time nor strength should be devoted to the actual details of calculation and disbursement, which were necessary in order to the maintenance of the material aspects of the fellowship.

I have drawn special attention to these simple and obvious facts, in order to leave upon the mind most definitely the true impression of the value of the word ministry, for it is of the utmost importance that this should never be lost sight of. Whatever developments we may presently have to consider, this quality persists. The idea of dignity, or of official importance, or prerogative, is entirely absent from the word itself. Of course there is a dignity in all service, there are prerogatives which appertain to service; but these result from the nature of the work to be done, and only exist in order that the work may be done thoroughly. Ministry connotes subservience, submission; and implicates necessarily, diligence and fidelity. This is clearly emphasized in the Apostles' declaration that in " the ministry of the Word " they would *continue stedfastly*, the phrase being the translation of one word, which signifies an earnest devotion to the business in hand, a pushing forward with strength in order to accomplishment.

This conception obtains in reference to both lines of service recognized in the paragraph under consideration, that of tables, and that of the Word. In each case the objective is the fellowship, the *kŏinōnia;* that sacred unity of Christ with His people, and their consequent union with each other. This fellowship is far more than an abstract idea. It is a living fact, and is to find expression in spiritual development and service, and in material well-being. The tables are for the carrying out of the latter; the Word is for the realization of the former. Hence the sacredness of the tables for the practice of fellowship. Hence the sacredness of the Word for the practice of fellowship. Hence also the sacredness of Ministry, whether of tables or of the Word.

Thus we see that the fundamental conception is that of diligent faithful devotion to an appointed work. Apart from that, there is neither dignity nor privilege attached to the work of Ministry. All this, I repeat, must never for a moment be lost sight of in our consideration of The Ministry of the Word, and much less in our exercise thereof.

We may now proceed to consider a development of the idea found in one outstanding passage in the apostolic writings. Before doing so however, and even at the risk of being charged with unnecessary repetition, let me insist upon

it, that development does not mean destruction
or change. It is rather the evolution of that
which is involved, the application of a persistent
principle to the supreme necessities of the work.
In the central idea of ministry with which we
have been dealing, there is no development, nor
can there be. Whatever the phase of ministry,
it always remains ministry, in the simplest and
therefore the final senses of the word. The development is in the method by which service is
rendered, and in its application to certain aspects of the one work.

The passage in which this development is
most fully dealt with in the New Testament is
found in Paul's letter to the Ephesians (Eph. iv.
1-13). Let us first take a broad view of the
passage, and then observe its particular revelation on this subject of ministry.

The passage opens the second part of the
letter, that in which the Apostle applied the
truths already enunciated, to the walk or behaviour of those to whom he was writing. The
keynote of the whole of this second section is
found in the words; "I . . . beseech you to
walk worthily of the calling wherewith we were
called." In order to this, and as the first condition of doing so, he urged them " to keep the

unity of the Spirit." This led him to write the passage in which that unity is so graphically set forth, and in the midst of which we find the idea of Ministry so fully developed.

In verses four, five, and six, we have a vision of the unity in itself. The organism is first described; "One body, and one Spirit, even as also ye were called in one hope of your calling." That is an inclusive description of the Church. It is one Body, Christ Himself being the Head, and all who share His life being members. His Body therefore has one life, that of the Spirit, Who is in the Head, and in the members, and thus unifies them in mind, and heart, and will, and power. This organism has one function, that of fulfilling the calling which the Apostle had described in the earlier part of his letter.

Next in order, and in the briefest but most pregnant phrases, we have an account of the generation of that organism; "One Lord, one faith, one baptism." The one Lord is Christ, as in the perfections of His Priesthood and Kingship, He is presented in the Gospel to the eye of men. The one faith is that of the repenting submission, and complete confidence, by which men yield themselves to Him as Saviour and Lord. The one baptism is that of the Holy

Spirit, which is the Divine response to human faith, and by which those who receive it are included in the Body whose function is that of the Divine calling.

Finally, the ultimate and resulting relation is described in the words; " One God and Father of all, Who is over all, and through all, and in all." The *all* refers in each case to the Head and members of the Body, that is to Christ and all believers; while the prepositions mark the different phases of relationship; the *of* is inclusive, the *over* marks sovereignty, the *through* signifies operation, and the *in* indicates communion.

Following this vision of the unity, there is a description of the growth of the organism, which occupies verses seven to thirteen. For the purposes of our present consideration we need only note the main statement which is discovered as we bring the seventh and thirteenth verses together; " Unto each one of us was the grace given according to the measure of the gift of Christ . . . till we all attain unto the unity of the faith, and of the knowledge of the Son of God, unto a full-grown man, unto the measure of the stature of the fulness of Christ."

A careful examination of the passage will

show that this bringing together of these verses is perfectly justified. All that lies between is of the nature of exposition of the phrase " the gift of Christ." The method of growth is that of the development of the gift of grace given to each member, in its relationship to the gifts of grace bestowed on all the rest. As all these are received and become operative, the whole Body grows towards its completion, towards the " full-grown man," towards " the measure of the stature of the fulness of Christ." Neither of these latter phrases applies to an individual Christian, but to the complete and perfected Church, which alone can realize " the stature of the fulness of Christ."

This brings us to the matter specially pertinent to our present consideration, that namely of Ministry. It is dealt with in the verses eight to twelve to which we have already referred as being expository of the phrase in the seventh verse, " the gift of Christ."

Having declared by quotation from the Psalms, that when Christ " ascended on high He led captivity captive, and gave gifts unto men "; and in a parenthesis having declared that His ascension followed His descension, and was an ascension to the place of supreme au-

thority, for the purpose of filling all things;—
the Apostle proceeded to speak of the gifts He
bestows, and to declare their purpose. Let us
first notice the purpose. It is stated in the
twelfth verse; " For the perfecting of the saints
unto the work of ministering, unto the building
up of the Body of Christ." Thus the gifts bestowed were in order to perfect the saints, in
order that they—the saints—might fulfil the
work of ministering. In that is included both
the ministry of tables and of the Word, in so
far as these are necessary to the building up of
the body of Christ; and necessarily also that
larger ministry which is the special vocation of
the Church both here and in the ages to
come.

It is of vital importance that we recognize
that the full ministry of the Church can only be
fulfilled by the whole Church, as that Church
consists in the unity of Christ with His members. Nevertheless in order that the Church
may fulfil that ministry, there is a ministry
within her organic life, which is created by gifts
which the Head bestows by the Spirit, to quote
from another of Paul's letters, " dividing to
each one severally even as He will."

These gifts are those of Apostles, Prophets,

Evangelists, and Pastors and Teachers. These are all in the Ministry of the Word.

When we come to consider more fully the primitive Ideal these will be dealt with more particularly. For the present study a general survey of the ground will be sufficient. The words themselves are suggestive, and may well be examined quite simply. The word Apostle is usually said to mean one who is sent. As a matter of fact its first meaning is that of being set apart. This we shall consider more particularly later. The word, as it was commonly used, referred to a delegate, an ambassador. Luke tells us that our Lord definitely selected the name for the Twelve, when He selected them. The word Prophet means a fore-teller, only we must bear in mind that the prefix *fore* has the sense of "in front of," and refers to place as well as time. The word Evangelist simply means one who tells good news. The final gift is indicated by the use of two words, Shepherd and Teacher, thus signifying a double function; the first in the realm of life, oversight, and sustenance; the second in the realm of knowledge, that of making known.

Such are the gifts, and they are all bestowed by the Head of the Church according to the good pleasure of His wisdom. The exercise of these gifts may now be described with equal brevity, and so the subject be reserved for fuller treatment.

The Apostle deals with the whole body of Truth. He has to state it, to systematize it, to make it available to the saints, in order to their guidance and sustenance.

The Prophet has to make the light of Truth shine in front of men. He is a man of Light and of Law.

The Evangelist has to apply the aspects of Truth which inspire hope. He declares the facts of the Evangel. He is a man of Life and Love.

The Pastor and Teacher receives the obedient, shepherds and instructs them in all the things of their life and service.

It is quite evident that these were separate gifts, but those receiving them were all called to Ministry, and once again the word must in each case be interpreted by the values which we discussed at the beginning.

A question arises as to whether these various gifts are ever merged in the experience of one man. We must not dogmatize, but personally I think they rarely are. They are sometimes changed in the course of a life-work. The business of every man is to define his gift, and then to make full proof of his ministry in its use. When this is done, the gifts are never in conflict, but make up a perfect coöperation of service.

Thus then it is seen that the fundamental conception of ministry within the Christian Church is that of service rendered in obedience to authority. This is equally true of the ministry of the whole Church, the ministry of Tables, and the ministry of the Word. Ministry is made possible by the bestowment of gifts by the One under Whose authority it is carried out.

Ministers then in every case, and so in that of the preaching of the Word, are servants of Christ. They owe to Him absolute and unconditioned allegiance. Therefore they are servants to none other, in the sense of submission to authority. They become servants of all, in the sense of doing their work on behalf of others. This is involved in the fact that they are the servants of Christ, Who said of Himself; " The Son of man came not to be ministered unto, but to minister, and to give His life a ransom for many." They take their orders only from Him, but those orders are ever such as compel them to serve the highest interests of others, while emptying themselves in the sacred work.

The conception of ministry then is full of heavenly dignity, but it is ever the dignity of self-emptying, and never that of self-aggrandizement. The minister of Christ is careless as to the opinion of all save his Lord, but he is full of care for the welfare of all those loved of his Lord.

In the secret place of his fellowship with his Lord, he will ever submit himself with all lowliness of mind, loyalty of heart, and submissiveness of will, in order that he may discover exactly what he is to say, where he is to go, and what he is to do. Then, as he passes out to obey those behests of his Master, he will do so without fear or faltering, in a consciousness of complete authority, and in the very spirit and behaviour of that gracious and unfathomable love, which is the inspiration of the authority under which he serves.

B

THE WORD

WE now come to the consideration of the second of the fundamental conceptions as it is suggested by the term "The Word." Here we are at once conscious of the necessity for the most careful attention. This term, "The Word of God," is in common use to-day. Sometimes it is employed with evident spiritual discernment; often I fear it must be said with great carelessness; and for the most part, even by devout souls, with scant knowledge. We constantly hear the Bible spoken of as the Word of God. Let me at once say that I am not for a moment suggesting that this is an improper designation, but I am sure that the significance of the term is not understood by many who thus employ it. Ask them in what sense the Bible is the Word of God, or how it happens that it is the Word of God, or what they mean when they call it the Word of

God; and their answers, constantly devout in intention, are, alas, often lamentably ignorant in statement. We at once assume that our phrase, "The Word," is a satisfactory abbreviation of this larger phrase, "The Word of God." It undoubtedly was so in the instance which we have considered. When the Apostles declared that they would give themselves to the ministry of the Word, they referred to the Word of God. What then, we inquire, is the Biblical interpretation of the phrase? For answer to that inquiry we shall first glance at the general Biblical use of the term, and then examine one outstanding passage of interpretation.

In the Old Testament the term which is the equivalent of *Lŏgŏs* in the New, is *Dâbâr*. A glance at a Hebrew Lexicon will show the persistence of this term in the Scriptures of the Hebrew people. The word means quite simply a matter as spoken of; not the matter only, not the speaking alone, but the truth as uttered. We shall see presently how near akin is the idea of the word to the simple meaning of the Greek word *Lŏgŏs*. This word *Dâbâr* occurs constantly in connection with the name of God, and so we find the perpetually recurring formula, "the Word of the Lord." The claim of the prophets to authority was persistently based on the declaration, " the Word of the Lord came." To these Hebrew thinkers that which they so described was Wisdom. Their philosophies did not begin by the asking of a question, but by the affirmation of God, and of His essential Wisdom. The Word of the Lord to them was that Wisdom, as He uttered it, or made it known.

When we turn to the New Testament we find that every writer uses the term *Lŏgŏs* in some form. It was especially the term of three of them, namely Luke, Paul, and John. It is at least interesting to observe in passing that Luke employed it seventy-four times, Paul fifty-six, and John forty-three. That I recognize is a very mechanical statement, but it has its value. Their use shows that the intention of the word is an almost exact equivalent of that of the Hebrew *Dâbâr;* a matter, or truth, as uttered. The outstanding passage of interpretation to which I refer is of course that of the prologue to the Gospel according to John, and to that we shall return immediately.

Let us tarry for a few moments, at least, with the term itself. In this connection it is interesting to observe certain facts about the three writers to whom we have referred. Luke was himself a Greek, and undoubtedly influenced by the methods of Greek thought. Paul was a Hebrew, but educated Hellenistically. John was in my judgment evidently profoundly influenced, ere he wrote his Gospel by Philo. All of them were perfectly familiar with the term as then employed.

In the early Greek philosophies the term *Lŏgŏs* stood for the rational principle of the universe, the word meaning an expression of thought, *and* the thought so expressed; never the one without the other. Philo definitely used the term as referring to God's revelation of Himself. The distinction between Philo and John was that Philo never thought or spoke of it as " made flesh." John used it in exactly the same way as Philo, always including that deepest conception, that the Word was not only the method of revelation, but also the matter revealed; but his central declaration was that " The Word was made flesh." In stating it, however, he never detracted in any way from the values of the eternal and spiritual conception. In other words, he did not qualify Christ by Philo, but rather fulfilled Philo by Christ.

Now let us proceed to consider as far as we are able, the full content of the phrase, " The

Word," to the ministry of which these men gave themselves. This we will do by glancing at John's passage; and by a statement based upon the Biblical conceptions.

The scope of these Lectures does not necessitate more than a glance at John's prologue. A matter of supreme importance however is, that the mind should be kept upon the persistence of the thought of "the Word" throughout that prologue. The thought ascends from the abstract idea to that of personality. For us, all the values are resident in the Person. That Person is seen in different relationships, but the identity does not change. He is variously "the Word," "the Only-begotten from the Father," "Jesus Christ," "the only-begotten Son"; but these descriptions apply to the same supreme matter, or to the same Person. In the course of the prologue, the Word is revealed in cosmic relationships; in relation to God; in relation to the whole creation; in relation to the processes of redemption; in relation to individual souls. But throughout, the Word is a Person; and the Person is the Word. The Person Who is the Word is seen in two principal relations, which may be described as eternal and temporal. This may best be shown by bringing together verses one and fourteen, and setting the three declarations of the one over against the three of the other;

"In the beginning was the Word."	"The Word became flesh."
"The Word was with God."	"Dwelt among us."
"The Word was God."	"Full of grace and truth."

Thus the Word, according to John, is fundamental and eternal Grace and Truth, for ever with God, and very God; but revealed in human nature, and so resident among the sons of men for their illumination and salvation.

This is the exhaustive statement of the exhaustless fact, to the service of which all those are devoted who are in "the Ministry of the Word." It is necessary however that we should seek some more detailed explanation of the conception, if we are to fulfil that ministry, and therefore we shall attempt to make a statement, which will carry us no farther; but may help us to a working understanding of the most glorious truth.

When we speak of the Word then, we employ an inclusive term, which has a fourfold value. I will state the four aspects, and then briefly consider each in separation.

The Word is Grace and Truth, essentially, absolutely; and in their relation to all things.

The Word is that Expression of Grace and Truth, which makes them comprehensible.

The Word is the Record of the Expression of Grace and Truth; which Record is at once the germ and norm of interpretation.

The Word is the Interpretation of the Record of the Expression of Grace and Truth, as they, through it, progressively unfold their meanings, and urge their claims.

This brief summary will at once help us to recognize the spacious glory of that, to the service of which, we are called. As a summary it is bare and cold, and that almost necessarily. All the manifold colours of the infinite glory of the Eternal God are merged in the phrase The Word of God. Who then can hope to be successful in definition? Nevertheless the merging of those colours is Light, and Light finally reveals all things except itself. In light, I can look at everything except light. If any-one doubts the accuracy of that statement, let him look at the world in the light of the sun, and then endeavour to look at the sun. The only way of seeing it, is through a glass dark-ened. Our summary is of the nature of that darkened glass. If it helps to a conception of the glory of the Word of God, it will serve our purpose.

The Word is Grace and Truth essentially. This is the sense in which the expression is used in the first sentences in the prologue of John. "In the beginning was the Word, and the Word was with God, and the Word was God." The reference is to the fact in its entirety, to Grace and Truth in a unity which is complete in itself. In that sense the Word is the sum total of Wisdom. In its inclusive potentiality it is all strength, that is the Truth of it; and all beauty, that is the Grace of it. That moreover is the full glory of the Father. Of the Person, John said; "We beheld His glory, glory as of an only-begotten from a father, full of grace and truth." The reference in the exposition which follows is to the relation of this eternal fact to phenomena. Phenomena are things of sight, things that appear, as Noumena are things of the mind. This was the thought of the writer of the letter to the Hebrews in the words: "What is seen hath not been made out of things which do appear." In other words, phenomena are the result and demonstration, not of phenomena, but of noumena; not of things which do appear, but of things not seen. " The ages "—which appear—" have been fashioned by the Word of God "—which essentially is of the mind. The Word of God therefore is the reason or meaning of things. There is nothing unrelated thereto. Everything is tested by it; and is known as true or false, good or bad, beautiful or ugly, wise or ignorant, by that abiding and unchangeable standard. That is the ultimate definition of the Word of God, and every other phase of meaning is related to it, and so gathers force and value from it.

In the second place, the Word of God is the expression of Grace and Truth. That is the sense in which the term is used in the second great statement in the prologue of John; " The Word became flesh . . . and dwelt among us . . . full of grace and truth "; and also in the phrase employed by Luke in his prologue, " eye-witnesses and ministers of the Word." That is the sense of the declarations with which the letter to the Hebrews opens, where the term does not occur, but where the thought is present, " God . . . hath . . . spoken unto us in His Son." The idea is that of giving such form to the eternal facts as will bring them within the compass of finite intelligence. In God they are infinite, and so they can only be known to God. If they are to be known to men they must be expressed. According to Biblical conceptions, this work of finding the form of expression is always that of the Holy Spirit. One of the most remarkable and illuminative passages in the Bible on that subject is found in Paul's first letter to the Corinthians (ii. 10, 11); "Unto us God revealed them through the Spirit, for the Spirit searcheth all things, yea, the deep things of God. . . . The things of God none knoweth save the Spirit of God." Whenever then the Word is to be expressed, it must be through the instrumentality of the Spirit.

In the opening sentences of the letter to the Hebrews, already referred to, the two methods by which the Word has found expression through this instrumentality of the Spirit are declared. In the past, God spoke to the fathers in the prophets, by divers portions and in divers manners. That is a most inclusive reference. Every aspect of truth made known, every gleam of grace outshining, all portions of the essential and eternal whole of the Word, came as God spoke. This He did in many manners; sometimes by direct and mystic communication with the soul; sometimes by clear and unmistakable interpretation of the events in the midst of which men lived; sometimes by lifting the soul into a realm of high exaltation, in which, apparently out of its own consciousness, it uttered songs of revealing and amazing beauty. By these and many other methods, the Spirit gave form and expression to the eternal Word as men were able to bear it.

It should be borne in mind that this method was not confined to the Hebrew people, although in them it had its great centre and most direct glory. There are many gleams of Grace and Truth in pagan literature. We do not need to turn to them however, for there is nothing in them not to be found in the literature which, as we shall presently see, God created in a peculiar way, not for the Hebrew people only, but for humanity.

The second part of the opening passage of the Hebrew letter tells of the central and final method by which the Word is expressed; "God . . . hath . . . spoken unto us in His Son." That is but another way of expressing the fact which John expressed in the words, "The Word was made flesh." By incarnation, the Word found its inclusive and perfect expression for man. In the Being of Jesus, through His Person, through His speech, and finally through the exodus He accomplished,—by the Cross, the resurrection, and the ascension,—all of Grace and Truth which man needs to know, or can know, found full and final expression.

In relation to that, it is well at once to say that the expression was far more wonderful than man has yet discovered. His understanding of it is gradual and progressive; and hence arises the necessity for the other phases of the Word to which we shall presently refer. Suffice it now for us to recognize the fact that the Word of God incarnate includes all the divers portions of the past; all the much more, which we have already apprehended; and still very much more, which we have yet to apprehend. Indeed, in a mystery far transcending our powers of explanation, so complete is the expression of the eternal Word in the Son of God, that Paul could only express his sense of it by inclusively declaring; "In Him dwelleth all the fulness of the Godhead corporeally."

Thirdly then, the Word is the record of the expression of Grace and Truth. In order that men might know and profit by the Speech of God, whether in the divers portions and manners of the past, or in the Son, it was necessary that the expressions should be preserved in such form that they might be at the disposal of men for all time. This was accomplished in the sacred Scriptures. In the second letter of Peter, we have a statement which reveals, so far as it is possible, the method by which these writings were produced (i. 21); "Men spake from God, being borne along by the Holy Spirit." In that statement we discover the natural and supernatural elements. Men spake from God. That is natural in the highest sense of the word. As they spake, in their own languages, in conformity with their own mental powers, influenced by their own surroundings, so also they wrote. But they were borne along by the Holy Spirit. The figure is that of a vessel with all sails stretched to the winds, and carried out beyond all the limitations which hold it, apart from that action of the wind, into the deeps. So these men, speaking and writing with all the simplicity of a perfect naturalness, were supernaturally guided into the most profound deeps; being thus inspired to say and write what should be said and written, and equally to omit the things which should be omitted. The result of this method, at once human and Divine, we have in our Bible. The Old Testament is the inspired literature of need, inquiry, hope; while the New is that of supply, response, possession. To deal with human need the Old Testament is necessary. To deal with God's answer the New is essential.

The value of this phase of the Word is that in these records of the expressions of the eternal Word of Grace and Truth, we have at once the germ and the norm of all revelation. We have the germ, waiting for interpretation, development, and persistent and progressive application. But we have the norm also, by which we test our speculations, theories, investigations. This is of central importance in the matter of our Christology. It is always perilous to attempt any other explanation of Him than that which adheres closely to the records. By so doing we inevitably sooner or later destroy Him, and proceed to the proclamation of a creature of our own futile speculations, rather than the Christ of God.

But there is yet another phase of meaning in the term " the Word of God." It is that of the persistent and ever growing interpretation of the records to which we have already incidentally referred. This also is of the Spirit of God, and as surely Divine and actual as anything with which we have already dealt. The Holy Spirit is ever available to those called to the ministry of the Word, in order to its explanation and application. The laws of the Spirit must be observed, and then He will definitely, immediately, and accurately, explain and interpret the writings. Thus the Word of God is still living and powerful.

But more. Because the Word must ever be incarnate in order to the illumination and saving of men, and because the saints are called upon to be witnesses, living epistles, the Spirit energizes the will, and enables the life, and thus all who obey become revelations of Grace and Truth.

This then is the Word, to the ministry of which we are called. To roughly summarize. The Word is eternal Grace and Truth; Grace and Truth expressed; the records of the expression of Grace and Truth; and the living interpretation of the records of the expression of Grace and Truth.

If this examination of the fundamental conception enshrined in the phrase, " The Word,"

II

The Primitive Ideal

A

THE WORD AS THE TRUTH OF THE APOSTLE

WE now turn to a more detailed consideration of the work of the Ministry of the Word as we find it revealed in the New Testament, in order that we may apprehend the primitive ideal. For the moment we resolutely ignore all modern conditions. To these we shall subsequently return; and we shall be able to deal with them the more intelligently in proportion as we have clearly seen these first things in the history of this ministry.

From this point onward in our consideration, the term "*the Word*" must be understood according to the interpretation already given. Specifically it always refers to one or other of the phases, and therefore involves all of them. Following the line suggested by the apostolic division of the work into four phases, we commence with that of the Apostle.

In a previous Lecture we have defined the apostolic functions broadly in these words;

The Apostle deals with the whole body of Truth. He has to state it, to systematize it, to make it available to the saints, in order to their guidance and sustenance.

In that definition we have employed the present tense, because the need of true apostolic work of this kind is perpetual; and, as we shall see later, the apostolic gift is still bestowed within the Christian Church. That we may be clear as to the nature and value of that gift, we now consider the New Testament teaching on the subject, dealing with; The Apostolic Gift; the Apostolic Function; and the Apostolic message or Truth. We shall endeavour to come to the New Testament without prejudice, in order to discover its teaching. Therefore we shall be elementary in our method.

Starting with the statement of Paul, " He gave some apostles," we have to discover the nature of this gift. We will begin with the word itself; and then deal with its place in the New Testament.

The word *apŏstŏlŏs* is a noun derived from the verb *apŏstĕllŏ*. Divesting our minds of all the ideas which we usually associate with the word,—which may be false or true,—we have to recognize that the fundamental conception is not that of sending, but of separation. This is very strongly so; and this lends force and meaning to the idea of sending. The action which makes an apostle is that of separating him from all other matters, in order that he may be devoted to one particular business; and that invariably, the business of the one who thus sets him apart. The ambassador who goes in the name of the king, to represent the king, and to transact the business of the king, is set apart to the work. This setting apart is the fundamental idea suggested by the word itself.

In use however, the word always refers also to the actual carrying out of the purpose for which the separation has taken place. The action is always that of the definite sending of the one separated; so that the apostle is always the messenger, separated in order to the fulfilment of a mission, and the one who carries out the mission. In the simplest sense of the word then, an Apostle is one who is rigorously set apart, in order to go on an embassy on behalf of the One Who separates him. The apostolic gift in the Christian Church is that Divine bestowment, which at once separates him who receives it to the doing of a certain clearly defined work; and perfectly equips him with all that is necessary for the doing thereof.

The use of the word in the New Testament is in strict accordance with these simple and fundamental intentions. The verb with its ordinary sense of " to send " is always used with the idea of very definite authority in the sending, and so also in the going. It is at least an interesting fact that the first time we come across the verb in the New Testament is in the statement that Herod *sent forth* and slew all the male children that were in Bethlehem. Here the fact of authority is clearly marked. The noun is employed almost invariably of the twelve disciples whom the Lord selected, separated, and sent. The exceptions are so few that we may name them. There are five in all, of which three are definite, and two are doubtful. The clear exceptions are; first, where the word is used of the Lord Himself (Heb. iii. 1); secondly, where in writing to the Philippians Paul spoke of Epaphroditus as *your apostle* (Phil. ii. 25); and finally, where in the Apocalypse we read of false apostles (Rev. ii. 2). The doubtful exceptions are; first, where our Lord used the word generally, but where possibly He was still referring to the Twelve

(John xiii. 16); and, where Paul referred to "our brethren the apostles of the Churches," in which case he may have been thinking still of the Twelve (2 Cor. viii. 23). In every other case the noun is used of the Twelve.

Let us now consider the use of the word in connection with the Twelve. Mark and Luke give a careful account of how the Lord definitely selected twelve from among the number of His disciples for specific work. In this connection Luke tells us that He named them Apostles. This is of great value as revealing the fact that this name was not one which they chose for themselves; nor was it one given to them by outsiders. There can be no question that our Lord selected it with a full sense of its deepest meaning, and in order to define clearly the nature of the gift He bestowed upon them, and of the work that they would be called to do.

In Mark's story of this choosing of the Twelve, he indicated the double nature of the appointment. They were appointed; first, to be with Him. This is the fundamental idea of separation. There were senses in which the rest of the disciples continued with Him; but in the case of the Twelve, there was a special separation from all other persons and business,

in order that in close association with Himself,
they might be prepared for the specific work
for which they were intended. They were appointed also "that He might send them forth
to preach." Here we find the verb *apostĕllō*
involving the separation, and indicating the
work which they had to do.

Mark and Luke give the names of the Twelve
in connection with their accounts of this election on the part of the Lord. Matthew, who
does not give this account, records the names
when he tells of their sending forth on their
first mission. The three of them, Matthew,
Mark, and Luke, in giving the story of their
sending forth, make use of the verb *apostĕllō*.
In each case it is evident that their specific and
central work was that of preaching. They were
sent by the Lord to proclaim His word, to deliver His message, to make known the Truth
about Himself. Certain powers were conferred
upon them, the exercise of which would serve
as signs, giving emphasis to their message.
These however were distinctly secondary in
importance, their chief responsibility being that
of the Word which they were to proclaim, the
understanding of which in their own case was
the result of their having been with Him.

After His resurrection from among the dead it was to these twelve He specially appeared in the upper room. Others were with them, on some occasions, and once at least He appeared to five hundred brethren. Luke in his second treatise, the Acts of the Apostles, lays special emphasis upon the fact that He gave commandment to the Apostles. He also tells how they asked Him whether He would at that time restore the Kingdom to Israel; and how He replied by a simple and yet inclusive definition of their responsibility. They were to be His witnesses in Jerusalem, in all Judæa and Samaria, and unto the uttermost part of the earth. This charge was in a particular and peculiar sense intended for the Apostles. While all believers are to be His witnesses, it was the duty of this apostolic band to state the Truth authoritatively. Hence we presently see the growing company of the disciples continuing steadfastly in the Apostles' teaching; and when Paul wrote his letter to the Ephesians we find him referring to them as constituting, with the prophets, the foundation, of which Jesus Christ Himself is the chief Corner-stone. It is thus that the Church of Christ is not catholic only; it is apostolic also. As these Apostles formulated the Christian doctrine under the guidance of the Holy Spirit, they fulfilled the true function of their apostleship. In this sense these men have had no official successors. Indeed they had no power or authority to appoint to the office. One of their first mistakes after their Lord had departed from them as to bodily presence, was that of choosing Matthias, when already the Lord had separated a man named Saul to make up the number of the first Twelve. In another sense they have always had successors, but to that we shall come presently.

So far we have only seen the idea as set forth in the history of the New Testament. We may now pass to a statement of the true apostolic function. What that function was in the case of the Twelve clearly emerges from that examination. They were specially called for the clear enunciation of Truth concerning the Lord Himself, and for the doing of this work they were specially prepared by their close association with Him. The principle upon which they proceeded to the election of a successor shows that they appreciated the importance of this, though they narrowed the conception of how this association was possible. Peter said; " Of the men therefore which have companied with us all the time that the Lord Jesus went in and out among us, beginning from the baptism of John, unto the day that He was received up from us, of these must one become a witness with us of His resurrection." The idea that an Apostle must have definite, first-hand knowledge of the Lord Jesus in order to witness concerning Him, was perfectly accurate. The mistake consisted in the narrow conception of the way in which that condition could be fulfilled. It was perfectly realized in the case of Saul of Tarsus by special revelation, notwithstanding the fact that he probably never saw his Master in the days of His flesh. All those called to apostleship were men who had direct, first-hand knowledge of the Lord, and who were thus prepared for the work of stating the Truth concerning Him.

This particular apostolic function is suggested by a statement found in the early part of the Acts of the Apostles. Under the preaching of Peter on the day of Pentecost about three thousand souls were added to the Lord. Of these Luke says that "they continued stedfastly in the Apostles' teaching, and fellowship, in the breaking of bread, and the prayers." In these words we have an account of the fourfold safeguard of the early Church. That safeguard is described by the use of four phrases, arranged in two couplets. "In the Apostles' teaching, and fellowship; in the breaking of bread, and the prayers."

Of these the first in order of statement was first also in importance, because it was fundamental. It was that of the Apostles' teaching. The word *didachē* here translated teaching, derived from *didaskō*, to teach, was used for instruction, both as to the act and the subject. It was in that respect kin of the word *lŏgŏs*, which as we said in our earlier studies meant the Word not only as an expression, but also as the truth expressed. There can be little doubt that in this particular passage the word had both meanings. These people continued steadfast in their attendance upon the actual teaching of the Apostles, and in their obedience to what they taught. The word occurs subsequently in the Book of the Acts. The Sadducean Sanhedrim charged the Apostles with having filled Jerusalem with their *teaching*, in spite of the fact that they had been straitly charged to remain silent (Acts v. 28). At Paphos, the pro-consul, Sergius Paulus, "believed, being astonished at the *teaching* of the Lord" (Acts xiii. 12). The men of Athens brought Paul to the Areopagus, and asked to be told what the new *teaching* was, which was spoken by Paul (Acts xvii. 19). All these references point to the same conception of a body of doctrine, or a statement of truth, concerning the Lord Himself, which it was the work of the Apostle to declare.

We may summarize our consideration of the function of the Apostle then by saying that he is a man chosen by Christ Himself; set apart to Christ, to be with Him for special knowledge of Him; sent by Christ, to deliver that very message of truth concerning Himself, which he has gained by this separation of comradeship and communion.

This brings us to the last phase of this consideration, that namely which is concerned with the apostolic message, or truth. In writing to the Ephesians, and in connection with his discussion of this subject of the ministry, Paul made use of a suggestive and revealing phrase, "As truth is in Jesus." In that phrase we have an inclusive description of the whole of apostolic teaching. Let us call to mind the statement in which the phrase occurs. Urging these Gentile believers to walk no longer as they had walked, he said; "Ye did not so learn Christ, if so be that ye heard Him, and were taught in Him,

even *as truth is in Jesus*." That had been the
nature of his apostolic teaching, believing
which, these people had entered into life. Let
the phrase be pondered, and its inclusiveness
and value will be discovered. Truth here stands
for that which is essential and eternal; the actual and the absolute truth. It is the word
which our Lord employed when He said of
Himself, " I am . . . the Truth "; and that
at once helps us to understand the full phrase,
" As the truth is in Jesus." The last five words
of the phrase constitute a sentence, which exactly describes the apostolic conviction, and reveals the scope of their teaching. The truth is
in Jesus. They had found that essential and
eternal truth had its final expression in Jesus.
Their teaching was the exposition of the truth
so expressed. To them was given the gift of
enabling them to state that truth in such form,
as to be the guide of all believers in their growth
" into Him Who is the Head, even Christ, from
Whom all the body fitly framed and knit together . . . maketh the increase of the body
unto the building up of itself in love."

We shall gain further important light on this
subject as we consider how these first Apostles
did their work. They first preached Jesus; that

is, they told the story concerning Him, as they knew it, of their own personal experience. Realizing that essential and eternal truth was expressed in Him, they presented Him to others as He had been presented to them. The whole method of apostolic declaration may be gathered from an examination of the first apostolic pronouncement, that of Peter on the day of Pentecost as it is recorded for us in the Book of the Acts (chap. ii.). He told the listening multitudes the simple yet inclusive story of Jesus; as a Man through Whom God wrought signs in His life, which showed Him to be approved of God; as One Who was delivered to death by the determinate counsel and foreknowledge of God, and slain by the men of Israel, by the hand of men without law, that is Gentiles; as having been raised and exalted by God; and as having shed forth the Holy Spirit upon all flesh. That is to say that Peter preached or proclaimed Jesus, and in so doing proclaimed Truth, and so fulfilled his apostolic ministry.

Thus the Truth of the Apostles was that of the Word of God, as it was in the beginning, and as it was spoken to men in Jesus. This was the first method and message of all the Apostles. In this first message, as in all subsequent ones preserved for us, it is to be observed that these men employed the writings of the Old Testament in their preaching of truth as it is in Jesus. They did not interpret Him by these writings, but rather these writings by Him; so proving at once their true value and their limitation.

As time passed on, they added writing to their preaching, and so under the guidance of the Spirit provided those new writings which complete the Old, as they give men for all time the truth concerning Jesus, and so embody the truth, "as the truth is in Jesus." Not all the Twelve wrote. Moreover some wrote who were not of the number of the Twelve. All the writings however were under apostolic influence, and were produced in the fellowship of the Apostles. This we shall see as we proceed.

Apostolic Truth then is found in our New Testament. It is the literature of Christ. There we hear Him, and are taught in Him, even as Truth is in Jesus. The subject from first to last is Jesus Christ the Word of God. Therefore this literature is in very deed the Word of God to us; and it is the apostolic Truth, which was once for all delivered by these Apostles to the Church.

It is not the purpose of this Lecture to deal

with these writings in detail, but it will be of
value to summarize their content.   In the first
four of them the subject is that of the Word of
God, as He appeared in human history.   Two
of these, those dealing with the Kingly and
Divine aspects of His Person, were written by
Apostles, Matthew and John.   The other two,
those presenting Him in His saving and human
aspects, were written by men under the influence of Apostles, and in fellowship with them;
Mark with Peter, and Luke with Paul.   Thus
the presentation of the Person is apostolic.
Then follow two and twenty writings in which
the Word of God is presented, as He is realized
and proclaimed through His mystical Body the
Church.   Of these the first is a picture, full of
life and colour from the pen of an artist, Luke,
who travelled and wrought in fellowship with
the great Apostle Paul.   In it, Christ the Word
is seen, moving out towards the uttermost parts
of the earth, through His Spirit-filled witnesses.
Then follow twenty-one letters and pamphlets,
which constitute a body of instruction for the
Church.   In the writing of these, three Apostles were employed, Paul, Peter, and John; and
two, James and Jude, who were the close associ-
ates of the apostolic band.   The one anony-

mous pamphlet, namely the letter to the Hebrews, is certainly apostolic in its teaching, and
was probably Luke's reproduction of Paul's
teaching.   At least that is as well-founded a
speculation as any other.   Thus the presentation of the Church is apostolic.   The subject of
the last writing is that of the Word of God, in
His personal glory, in His relation to His
Church, and in His governmental procedure,
whereby He establishes the Kingdom of God on
earth.   This was written by the Apostle John.
Thus the final writing is also apostolic.

Thus then is revealed the apostolic message.
It was, and is essentially, that of the Word; that
is, the Whole of Truth as it was embodied and
expressed in the Son of God, as the Son of man.
In the apostolic writings we have that Truth
stated, systematized, and applied.   These writings then constitute at once the germ and norm
of all apostolic preaching.   They are the germ,
needing development and progressive application.   They are the norm, by which all developments and applications must be tested, lest they
depart from the Truth.

While the number of the foundation Apostles
was completed, and in these writings we have
the full body of apostolic doctrine, it is never-

theless true that the apostolic gift is still needed
and bestowed.   It is needed wherever the Word
is to be given to a people in a new tongue, or to
meet new conditions.   The work of translation,
which is too often looked upon as being merely
academic, is strictly apostolic.   When we remember the great translators, that will be conceded.   The work of the true theologian is also
distinctly apostolic.   It is that of stating the
eternal truth in the new terms of the new age;
and that without destroying its essential character.   For the doing of this work also, no merely
academic equipment is sufficient.   The gift of
the Apostle is necessary.

From this interpretation it will be seen that
the apostolic is one phase only of The Ministry
of the Word.   There is a sense in which all
Christian ministry is apostolic, whereas all
Christian ministry is not necessarily prophetic,
nor evangelistic, nor pastoral and didactic.   All
ministry of the Word is apostolic, because it is
concerned with the Truth, which received apostolic interpretation under the guidance of the
Spirit, and must always be tested by that interpretation.   In this sense apostolic ministry is
fundamental and continuous.   There are prophets, evangelists, pastors and teachers, who have

not the apostolic gift, but all of them have to do with this apostolic teaching. It is the bond of union between them. The proportion in which this fact is realized, is the proportion in which any sense of conflicting interest in the exercise of this ministry, as between those of the different orders, is impossible. Each in his own order will recognize the complementary nature of all the orders, and there will be perfect co-operation.

In this connection I may be permitted to say how out of place the word succession is, in reference to the Christian ministry. There is no such thing as Apostolic succession, as there is no such thing as Prophetic, or Evangelistic, or Pastoral succession. The call to the ministry is personal and direct; and for the equipment of those called, gifts and grace are supplied not mediately, but immediately, by the Head of the Church, through the Holy Spirit.

The historic continuity and unity of the Christian ministry is maintained by The Word of God, which liveth and abideth for ever. The gifts vary, and the secondary means by which they are received are more perhaps than we have recognized. They were bestowed in New Testament times by the laying on of hands, sometimes by bishops, or presbyters, sometimes by the members of the Church; and so they still undoubtedly are, as bishops and Christian believers act under the Lordship of Christ. In those days they were received without any laying on of hands, and so they still undoubtedly are.

That which mattered then, and that which matters yet, is the Truth of which the Apostles were, and are, the interpreters. The testing of Apostolic ministry therefore is that of the Truth itself. If one claiming apostolic gifts and functions denies the faith once for all delivered to the saints, his claim is disproved by that denial.

Thus the sacredness of the work of Apostolic ministry of the Word is revealed.

B

THE WORD AS THE BURDEN OF THE PROPHET

WE now turn to the second phase of the ministry of the Word referred to by the Apostle, that namely of the Prophet. We have already broadly defined the term Prophet as referring to one whose office it is; *To make the light of Truth shine in front of men; he is a man of light and of law.*

The work of the Prophet in the Christian economy is always dependent upon that of the Apostle. In his first letter to the Corinthians, Paul explicitly stated this, when he wrote; "God hath set some in the Church, first apostles, secondly prophets, thirdly teachers"[1] (1 Cor. xii. 28). This does not mean that the Apostle occupies a higher rank than the Prophet

---

[1] The reason for the omission of the Evangelist here probably is that the Apostle was dealing with the gifts of value within the Church, rather than with the one by which men are brought into the Church. Whereas the work of the Prophet has application beyond the Church, it also has values within, and so was included.

or Teacher. Such an idea of rank is wholly of this world, and has no place in Christian organization.

In considering this subject of the prophetic gift we must give particular attention to the idea as it is found in the New Testament. It is to say the least, an interesting and suggestive fact, that the word prophet is far more common there than the word apostle. I confess that this fact surprised me when I noticed it—but it is so.

In the New Testament writings we find a group of words, all based upon one central idea. To understand the true nature of prophetic ministry, we must discover that idea. In order to do so, we shall again come to these writings with an open mind, endeavouring to find the conception, apart from all foregone conclusions. We will follow the same method, considering; the Prophetic Gift; the Prophetic Function; and the Prophetic Burden.

The central word of the group referred to is the word Prophet, employed by the Apostle in his statement, " He gave . . . some prophets." Our word prophet is really a transliteration of the Greek word *prophētēs*, which also appears in the feminine form *prophētis*, rendered prophetess. This is a compound word, made up of the prefix *prō*, which means fore, in the sense of in front of, or before; and the verb *phēmi*, to speak. This verb, which literally means to show, or make known, is derived from *phainō*, to shine.

This very elementary method of consideration gives us the simplest and the truest value of the word itself. According to it, the Prophet is one who makes Truth known to men in such a way that it arrests the attention. He is one through whose ministry the Truth shines forth upon men, so that they find themselves in its light. While the Apostle is chiefly concerned with the Truth in itself, the Prophet is concerned with its statement to men in such terms that it may make its proper appeal to them. The whole emphasis is on the Truth, as made known, as shining forth, as applied. While the Apostle is called to state the essential and eternal Truth, as it found expression in Jesus, the Prophet is supremely called to show the bearing of that Truth on temporal things. In prophetic ministry we find therefore what we may describe, for lack of a better term, as the tenses of Truth. It deals with the past, as it makes history the vehicle through which eternal principles have been revealed. It deals with the present, as it measures the things of to-day by eternal standards. It deals with the future, as it declares things to come, in order that the unveilings may produce an immediate effect upon the conceptions and conduct of men.

As we have said, this phase of ministry is constantly referred to in the New Testament. In addition to the words already cited, we find these cognate forms; *prŏphētĕuō*, to prophesy; *prŏphētĕia*, a prophecy; and *prŏphētikŏs*, prophetic. A study of all the passages in which these words are found makes it evident that the idea was taken over from the old economy, and from the writings of the Old Testament. To them, then, we may properly turn for an interpretation of the idea.

The Hebrew word for prophet is derived from a verb which means to speak or sing by inspiration. By inspiration here, I mean supernaturally; the speech or the song resulting from some Divine influence operating through the speaker or singer. There is nothing in the word which suggests the method of inspiration, but it stands for such speech, whether it deals with past, present, or future, as results from a Divine action, whereby the speaker utters, not his own private interpretations of events or

problems, but the Word of the Lord **concerning**
them.   The whole conception of prophesying
was that of proclaiming the thoughts of God;
and therefore the Prophet was always the instrument through whom God made known His
will to men.

The Old Testament conception moreover,
was ever that of the practical and ethical value
of prophecy.   The Old Testament Prophets
never spoke or wrote merely to satisfy curiosity,
either in their historic records, in their direct
messages, or in their foretelling of things to
come.   The purpose of their ministry was ever
that of producing immediate results in the lives
of those to whom their words were addressed.

I pause to stress this fact, because a common
use of the word shows how sadly it has been lost
sight of.   Constantly the word prophet is used
as though it referred to one able to predict coming events, and prophecy is conceived of as con-
sisting wholly of such predictions.   Moreover
altogether too often the study of the predictive
elements in Biblical prophecies degenerates into
a curiosity which is morbid, and often irrever-
ent, a desire to know " times and seasons," simply for the satisfaction which such knowledge
produces.

Nothing can be more erroneous. That the predictive element existed in prophetic ministry in the Hebrew economy, no one denies. Indeed it was the element which most clearly set the seal of the supernatural upon that ministry. This is clearly seen in the Book of Isaiah, where the Prophet makes this fact of prediction the proof of Divine authority, as he challenges the false gods and prophets; "Declare the things that are to come hereafter, that we may know that ye are gods. . . . Who hath declared it from the beginning that we may know? and before time, that we may say, He is righteous? yea, there is none that declareth . . ." (Isa. xli. 23 and 26). Yet even here, and always, the purpose of prediction was that of producing immediate moral results, and not that of affording intellectual satisfaction. This element was only one however, and if we may measure its value by its amount, it was the least important. Prophecy was also the interpretation of history. That is why all the historic books of the Old Testament were included in the Division which they named "The Prophets." Their historians were Prophets, because they ever set history in relation to the government of God, showing through it, how all disaster had resulted from disobedience to the Law of God, and all success from conformity thereto. Prophecy was also the interpretation of the will of God to men immediately, the inspired utterance which made known to men what was at the very moment the Divine purpose and way.

This complete conception of the prophetic office was taken over by the men of the new age. This fact must be borne in mind in any attempt to understand the gift of the Prophet. Prophecy is truth spoken, as the result of Divine inspiration, and with a view to producing Divine results in human affairs. The work of the Prophet is that of making such truth known to men in ways which command attention.

Let us now observe the idea as it is found in the New Testament, dividing our examination into two parts; first the references prior to Pentecost; and secondly, those afterwards. In both cases we find that references are constantly made to the Old Testament prophets. There is a sense of course in which the writings which record the things before Pentecost are post-pentecostal. That is to say, that probably none of them was written before the coming of the Spirit. Hence we find the constant statement that the predictions of the Prophets of the old economy were fulfilled in the life and death and resurrection of Jesus. All such references are of great value, not only as they reveal the relationship between the Hebrew and Christian economies, but also as they serve to show the true nature of Hebrew prophecy. In our examination I propose to confine myself to those references which deal with the prophetic gift within the Christian age.

The references to the ministry of the Prophet within the Christian era in the Gospels are few, but they are suggestive. Matthew gives us a fuller account than any of the other Evangelists of the ordination of the Twelve as they were sent forth on their first mission (Matt. ix. 35–x. 42). Here we find our Lord's charge to them. It is quite evident that as He spoke to them He was looking on to all the processes of the age which He was then inaugurating. The first part of the charge had to do with their immediate mission (Matt. x. 5–15). The second part covered the period from His ascension to the destruction of Jerusalem (x. 16–23). The final part dealt with the whole period thence, to the consummation of the age (x. 24–42). In the closing sentences of that final section He said, " He that receiveth a Prophet in the name

of a prophet, shall receive a Prophet's reward"
(ver. 41).

The only value of these words for the purpose
of our present study is, that they show that our
Lord deliberately indicated His adoption of the
prophetic method of ministry in connection with
the complete ministry of witness, to which His
people were to be sent forth.   At the close of
His ministry He uttered the final doom of the
city of Jerusalem. This was preceded by His
woes against the rulers, at the close of which He
said, " Behold I send unto you Prophets, and
wise men, and scribes; some of them shall ye
kill and crucify; and some of them shall ye
scourge in your synagogues, and persecute from
city to city " (Matt. xxiii. 34).   Here His reference undoubtedly was to the ministry of His
witnesses which would follow His departure,
and again we have evidence of His recognition
of the prophetic method. He employed the
term in reference to His own ministry when He
said, " A Prophet is not without honour, save in
his own country, and in his own house " (Matt.
xiii. 57); and the people spoke of Him as a
Prophet. These are the references to a Christian ministry of prophecy in the Gospels. They
are few, but they suffice to show that it was

within the intention of the Lord Himself that there should be such a phase of ministry. When we turn to the more strictly post-pentecostal times, we find a much more frequent occurrence of the idea.

In the Acts the prophetic character of pentecostal preaching emerges in the first apostolic declaration. When Peter interpreted the signs of the Spirit to the inquiring multitudes, he quoted the prophecy of Joel, declaring that it found its fulfilment on that day. According to that foretelling of the Hebrew Prophet, one of the great results of the outpouring of the Spirit would be that of the new age of prophecy which would then begin (Acts ii. 17, 18, 19). When, centuries before, the news was brought to Moses that Eldad and Medad were prophesying, he had exclaimed; " Would God that all the Lord's people were Prophets " (Num. xi. 29). From the hour when the great lawgiver breathed the wish, we pass to the days when Joel declared it would be realized, and so on to Pentecost when it was fulfilled.

While it is true that the Spirit equips all believers for prophetic witness, it is also true that there are those who have a special gift, and this is seen in the Acts. When the new movement was about to begin from Antioch, Prophets went down there from Jerusalem, and one of them, Agabus, uttered the predictive word concerning the great famine (Acts xi. 27, 28). This man appears again in the account of Paul's stay at Cæsarea, and again his message was predictive (Acts xxi. 10, 11). In the Church at Antioch Prophets were found (Acts xiii. 1). Judas and Silas are distinctly named as Prophets (Acts xv. 32). At Ephesus the gift of the Holy Spirit was signalized by the exercise of prophetic ministry (Acts xix. 6). The four daughters of Philip the evangelist prophesied (Acts xxi. 9).

In his first Corinthian letter Paul gave explicit instructions concerning the exercise of the prophetic gift.

All this is of value as it shows that the particular method of the Prophet in the ministry of the Word obtained in the earliest days of the Christian economy, and that it was one of the gifts bestowed within the Church, by the Head of the Church, through the Spirit.

The prophetic function emerges clearly into view in our consideration of the gift itself. In the second letter of Peter however, we have a statement which is of the utmost value in order to an accurate apprehension of the peculiar nature of prophesying. He was dealing with the experience on the Holy Mount, and especially with the influence which the voice, those who were present then heard, had upon them with regard to the prophecies of the past. The passage is so important that we quote it in full. " We have the word of prophecy made more sure; whereunto ye do well that ye take heed, as unto a lamp shining in a dark place, until the day dawn, and the day-star arise in your hearts; knowing this first, that no prophecy of Scripture is of private interpretation. For no prophecy ever came by the will of man; but men spake from God, being moved by the Holy Ghost " (2 Pet. i. 19–21).

Through the testimony of the voice of the Holy Mount to the Son of God, these men came to a new understanding of the nature of the prophetic writings, with which they had been familiar from childhood. These writings were, by this experience, made more sure to them. With that aspect of Peter's message we are not now interested, save in so far as it throws light upon the prophetic function. We have already seen that the idea in the New Testament is identical with that in the Old. All that is here said concerning the prophecies of the past is equally true concerning prophetic ministry to-day.

The function of prophecy then, is that of speaking the Word of God, that Word being received from God by the ministry of the Holy Spirit. The Prophet is not one who observes his age and gives his own interpretation of it. He is one who is carried along by the Spirit into a place of vision and understanding, above and beyond his age, from which he sees it as God sees it, and in which he receives from God the very message the age needs to hear. Such messages constitute light in dark places, to which men do well that they take heed.

Prophets then are men who are sure, because they are Spirit-taught; and they speak therefore with the note of absolute authority. The effect of their speaking may be that of condemnation, or of direction, or of inspiration. It is always practical, ethical, spiritual. All this will become yet clearer as we turn to the consideration of the Burden of the Prophet.

The word *burden,* in relation to prophetic ministry, is strictly an Old Testament word, and it has no exact equivalent in the New. Nevertheless we employ it, and are justified in doing so, because, as we have seen, the whole conception of prophetic ministry is carried over from the Old Testament into the New.   We will go back then to the Old in order to discover the meaning and use of the word there.   The Hebrew word (*Massâ*) literally means a burden or a load in our ordinary every-day sense.   It is used of the weights carried by beasts, and of responsibilities resting upon men.   The Prophets themselves appropriated the word, and made it the peculiar vehicle by which they expressed their own conception of the nature of their messages.   In their use of it, we find it stood for the truth made known to them by God; for the desire which they experienced to utter the truth; and for the message as they delivered it.   We now employ the word strictly in this sense.

The Burden of the New Testament Prophet, like that of the Old, is first the Truth made known by God in order that it may be declared to men.   Such truth, so made known to the Prophet, becomes a burden of desire, compelling him to utter it.   The message which, under such constraint, is proclaimed to men is the Word of the Lord.

What then is the Burden of the New Testament Prophet?   We may find a practically com-

plete answer to that inquiry in the words of
Peter in the house of Cornelius. At the close
of the address delivered when he perceived that
the Gospel was for the Gentile as well as the
Jew, he said, "To Him bear all the Prophets
witness." While these words are usually employed as though they referred to the prophecies of the past; and while such interpretation
of them is undoubtedly correct as far as it goes;
it is equally certain that they describe, and with
even more accuracy, the burden of Christian
prophesying. If the whole of that brief but
pregnant address be read, this will be the more
readily acknowledged. After telling the story
of Jesus in a very few words, he declared that
God had charged them "to preach unto the
people that this is He Which is ordained of God
to be the Judge of quick and dead." To Him
then, all the Prophets give witness. They declare His absolute sovereignty over all human
souls, whether quick or dead. Such declaration ever involves the illustration of that sovereignty; interpretation of its reasons, its
methods, its purposes; and application of the
one central fact to the circumstances in the
midst of which the Prophet is called to exercise
his ministry.

Some further light may be obtained from the passage in Peter's second letter to which we have already referred. Referring to the experience of the Holy Mount, he said; " We did not follow cunningly devised fables when we made known unto you the power and coming of our Lord Jesus Christ " (2 Pet. i. 16). The positive note in that statement is full of light. The whole burden of prophetic ministry is expressed in the words " the power and coming of our Lord Jesus Christ." They cover the whole fact of His relation to the world. In the next two sections of this letter he dealt with the perils threatening these truths. First the perils threatening the truth of the Power (chap. ii.). Carefully observe that this peril consisted in false prophets and teachers denying the Master. Then the peril threatening the truth of the Coming (chap. iii.). Again observe that this peril consisted in the mocking of those who disbelieved the predictions of the holy Prophets and the teaching of the Apostles. True prophecy then is that which proclaims His Power and His Coming; and such prophecy is ever of the nature of a lamp shining in a dark place.

Returning for a moment to a more abstract matter, it is interesting to turn to a passage

in Jeremiah, in which terrible things are written
against false prophets (xxxiii. 9–40). Towards
the close of that passage the whole question of
the use and abuse of the word burden is discussed. In the course of the discussion, the
human questions to which the prophetic burden is the true answer are given. They
are these; "What hath the Lord answered?"
"What hath the Lord spoken?" A real
prophetic burden then is the answer to
those questions; and the Prophet is the man
who answers them. In the light of that statement we turn to the letter to the Hebrews;
"God having of old time spoken unto the fathers in the Prophets by divers portions, and in
divers manners, hath at the end of these days
spoken unto us in His Son" (Heb. i. 1, 2). The
Son then is the One Prophet of God, and all
Prophets in the Christian age are such as give
the answer of His truth to humanity as it in-
quires, "What hath the Lord spoken?"

Thus then is clearly revealed the Burden of
the Christian Prophet. It is that of the Word
of God, embodied in the Word incarnate, the
Son in Whom God has spoken to all men and all
ages, everything that it is necessary that they
should know in order to the realization of the

purpose of God, which is also that of the true and glorious destiny of humanity.

This Word the Prophet is to declare, to apply, to insist on. His ministry is not that of the Apostle, not that of the Evangelist, nor that of the Pastor and Teacher. As we have seen, the work of the Apostle is ever that of giving all his attention to the Truth itself. The Prophet must receive the Truth from the Apostle. His prophesying in that sense must be apostolic. As we shall see, the work of the Evangelist is that of perpetually proclaiming the first things of the Truth; while that of the Pastor and Teacher is that of instructing the members of the Church in Truth, that they may grow thereby. The Prophet is rather the man who addresses his age, declaring to it the crown rights of the Lord, and showing how they affect all the affairs of men. It is a great ministry, full of infinite variety, charged with solemn responsibility, and yielding results which can never be expressed in human statistics. The voice of the Prophet will often be silenced by the clamour of opposition, but his word will abide, and being the Word of God, will never return to Him void.

The gift has persisted throughout the

Christian era, and it is still needed. Whether they will hear or whether they will forbear, men must still be compelled to attend to the proclamation of the truth about themselves, and about life, which Truth is all contained in the Word of God, which found its complete utterance in His Son.

That there have been, and still are those on whom this specific gift is bestowed will, I think, be readily conceded. Their preaching is ever characterized by national and social applications, rather than by individual appeal. That is not to say that it has no personal value. It certainly has, for the true Prophet never forgets that the nation consists of the People, and that the People, as a Commonwealth, is strong or weak in proportion as the individuals making up the whole are strong or weak. But it does mean that the Prophet is a man who sees clearly the whole movement of human life, and his message has to do with all human inter-relationships, and responsibilities, as these are conditioned within the Will of God. The Prophet therefore is not called upon to tarry with individuals. That is the work more specifically of Evangelists and Pastors and Teachers. Neither is he called upon to systematize the Truth.

That is the work of the Apostles. He, knowing this Truth, and realizing the fact that men are only perfected as they fulfil the Divine ideal of society, speaks to them as a whole. He will talk to them of history, ignoring the accidental incidents, as he interprets the fundamental and essential things of Divine law and rule. He will speak to every present situation, not discussing it from the standpoint of human observation, but declaring the Divine thought and purpose. He will foretell the way of God with men in the days to come, so far as that is revealed in the Scriptures, carefully avoiding all personal speculation as to details unrevealed.

The ministry of Prophets is always needed, but especially so in days of upheaval and breakdown in human affairs. Then, to men at their wits' end, he is called upon to proclaim the Word of the Lord, as it is found in the Son of God. By so doing he will give direction to men, following which, they will be able to build again the waste places, and realize all the possibilities of human society as they are known to God.

C

THE WORD AS THE GOSPEL OF THE EVANGELIST

THE third phase of the Ministry of the Word referred to by the Apostle is that of the Evangelist. In dealing with the subject of the Ministry, generally, we thus defined his work; *The Evangelist has to apply the aspects of Truth which inspire hope. He declares the facts of the Evangel. He is a man of Life and Love.*

In turning to a more careful examination of the subject we are at once arrested by the word itself. As in the case of the word prophet, the word Evangelist comes into our language by transliteration. That of course is true also of the word Apostle. The Greek word *ĕuaggĕlistēs* has become evangelist. The arresting fact however is that this is a new word in the Greek language, unknown apart from the Christian fact. It is Biblical and ecclesiastical, the word of the Bible and the Church. Derived from well-known words, all of which how-

ever acquired new meaning in their Christian
use, this particular word, describing the men
called to the definite work of proclaiming the
Gospel, was created for this sacred use. Again
we shall follow the same method of consideration, dealing in turn with, The Evangelistic
Gift, The Evangelistic Function, and The Evangelistic Gospel.

In dealing with the gift referred to by the
Apostle in his statement that " He gave . . .
some Evangelists," we will once more give attention to the suggestiveness of the new Testament group of words connected with the idea.
They are three; first, *ĕuaggĕlizō*, that is to
evangelize, or to preach the Gospel; second,
ĕuaggĕliŏn, that is the Evangel, or the Gospel;
and third, *ĕuaggĕlistēs*, that is the Evangelist.
Of these the second two are derivatives of the
first; while that is a compound of two words,
ĕu, good; and *aggĕllō*, to bring tidings, or to
announce. Thus to evangelize is to proclaim
good tidings; the Evangel is the message of
good tidings; while the Evangelist is the one
who proclaims good tidings. The central conception of the words is that of a message sent,
by someone to someone. That conception is
qualified by the word *ĕu*, meaning good or glad,

and gives character to the thought, as it suggests that it is a message which the sender is glad to send, and the receiver will be glad to receive.

When we turn from the words in themselves to their use in the New Testament, we find that all these conceptions are present, and are intensified and made superlative by the nature of the Message which is to be proclaimed. The strength of the idea everywhere is twofold. The first element is that of the goodness of the news. It is news such as to bring joy to the heart of those who hear it. It is tidings of great joy to all people. The greatness of it, and the gladness of it thrill and throb through every reference to it, and constitute the first element of its strength. The second element is that of the fact that it is sent. It is news from God, and He sends it to men. Therein is a revelation of His attitude towards men in their need, in their sin, in their sorrow. His purpose for them is that of goodness, and He has news for them of how that purpose may be fulfilled. That good news He has sent to them. These facts make the Evangel, the Gospel, the message from God, of the utmost importance, of the first urgency, of supreme delight. It is important because it is the message of God; urgent because it has to do with human need; and delightful because it is good news, news that tells of a way of deliverance from all that harms and hurts.

The Gospel is variously described in the New Testament writings, and the phrases are in themselves interesting and illuminative. In the Gospels we read of " The Gospel of the King-dom of God "; in the Acts of " The Gospel of the Grace of God "; in the Epistles of "The Gospel of God," and of "The Gospel of Christ"; in the Apocalypse of " an eternal Gospel." It may be that these phrases have dispensational values, that is that they suggest the various applications of the Gospel to various ages, or periods. With that aspect of their significance I am not now interested. That which impresses me is the unveiling I find in them of different aspects of the one Gospel, for finally there is but one Gospel. In the phrase " the Gospel of the Kingdom of God," I hear the note of authority. The good news cannot be doubted, for it is a royal proclamation, coming with all the majesty of the Throne behind it. The phrase " The Gospel of the Grace of God " at once reminds me that the King is merciful and full of compassion, and I know that the good news is a message of infinite and unfathomable Love. The phrase "The Gospel of God" calls back to the mind the fact that the King is God, that the Lover is God, and so makes the sense of the authority of the good news absolute, and the consciousness of the love, such as to banish all doubt. The phrase "The Gospel of Christ" speaks of the availability to man of all the grace promised in the message, for He is the Anointed of the Father, both as King and Priest, so that through Him men may find their way into the Kingdom through His Saviourhood. Such are the general impressions made by the prevalent idea in the New Testament writings. Let us take time to consider a little more particularly the place of the idea therein.

Here I begin with some incidental but none the less interesting and illuminative notes. The idea is not of frequent occurrence in Matthew; the verb being found once, and the noun four times. In Mark the noun only is found; it is however the very key-note of his story, as witness the opening phrase, "The beginning of the Gospel of Jesus Christ." In Luke the verb only is found; he being supremely concerned with the proclamation. John never employs either term save in the Apocalypse, where the noun is found twice. In the Acts it is found more frequently, the verb predominates, the noun occurring twice, and the word Evangelist once. In the letters of Paul the idea is constant, and the use of both noun and verb is common; the word Evangelist is found twice.

In the historic sequence of the mission of our Lord we find the word Evangel first used by Gabriel in his message to Zacharias concerning the birth of John the forerunner. " I was sent to speak unto thee, and to bring thee this *evangel*." It was used again by an angel of the Lord as he said to the shepherds, " Behold, I bring you an *evangel* of great joy which shall be to all people." Describing the preaching of the herald John, Luke employs it as he says, " With many other exhortations preached he the *evangel* unto the people." Mark, describing the commencement of the more public preaching ministry of the Lord, says, "Jesus came into Galilee, preaching the *evangel* of God." In the Acts the reference first in order to this aspect of ministry is found in the words, "And every day, in the temple and at home, they ceased not to teach, and to *evangelize* Jesus as the Christ."

These are but illustrations, and are given to show how this conception of evangelization characterized the ministry of John, of the Lord Himself, and of His earliest messengers. They all went out among men with the joyful assurance that they had good news to tell them.

As we carefully follow the revelation through the history, and through the writings, we cannot fail to observe the growing apprehension of the content and value of the Gospel, which came to these men. They came to think and speak of it as a glorious Gospel, a Gospel proceeding from the happy God,—for so we may read the words, " the ever-blessed God." They found it to be a lonely Gospel; if men preached other gospels they were not gospels, for there was but this one. They proved as they preached it, that it was a powerful Gospel, of which not to be ashamed, even in Rome. They realized growingly that it was a testing Gospel, dividing men as they heard it, into two distinct classes, those of believers, and unbelievers, and so those elected to life and glory, and those doomed to death and shame; the division and electing resulting from their response to the message.

The gift of the Evangelist is that special qualification which fits a man for proclaiming that good news to men powerfully and prevailingly. He gave—and He gives—some Evangelists.

The evangelistic function then is patently that of proclaiming this Gospel. Its special emphasis in the commission of our Lord is found in that recorded by Mark,[1] "Go ye into all the world, and preach the Gospel to the whole creation" (Mark xvi. 15). In this phrase "preach the Gospel" the verb *ĕuaggĕlizō* is not employed. The noun *ĕuaggĕliŏn* is preceded by the verb *kērussō*, which means to proclaim as a herald, or simply to herald. The command is to herald the good news. Thus the phrase is rich in its revelation of the function of the Evangelist. The command to herald the Gospel gives the note of authority to evangelistic preaching. It speaks of the authorizing King; considers the message as authorized; and thus creates the authority of the messenger. This aspect of the work of the Evangelist implicates the claim of God upon man, and the consequent duty of man towards the message which God sends. While the message is one of infinite grace, good news indeed;

---

[1] The commission as recorded by the four Evangelists must not be confounded. See my *Missionary Manifesto*.

it comes from the King, and therefore it is not one which man can treat lightly. Upon his reception of it, issues of tremendous and age-abiding importance depend. If the Prophet comes to men with the authoritative formula, "Thus saith the Lord," so also does the Evangelist, and this he will never forget. He offers a message of incomparable grace, but it is the proclamation of eternal government, with which men must not trifle. Indeed the one sin which has no forgiveness is that of refusing to believe the message, and so resolutely declining the Divinely appointed way of deliverance.

But we return again to the other word of the phrase. It is the Evangel which is thus to be heralded. The King sends a message, but it is a message of Love. The eternal Government issues its proclamation, but it is a proclamation of Grace, offering pardon, deliverance, restoration of all forfeited rights and privileges. This aspect of the work of the Evangelist implicates the need of man, and the Grace of God. And this is the supreme matter. The function of the Evangelist is not that of denouncing sin; nor is it that of discussing judgment in the sense of punishment. Both these things he will certainly have to do in the course of his preaching,

but he cannot end with them. They are not
the things he is specifically called upon to do.
He is sent to sinning men, to men under sentence of punishment, to tell them of God's provision for their forgiveness, cleansing, deliverance. The Evangelist then comes ever with
joy and gladness. He is a man alive with the
tremendous fact that God has found a way by
which His banished ones may return; and his
preaching must ever be vibrant with the passionate joy of it in his own soul. A gloomy,
pessimistic Evangelist is a contradiction of
terms. An Evangelist, cheerful even to hilarity,
and optimistic in spite of the most utter hopelessness in human thinking, is in the natural order. The Evangelist goes out in faith, in love,
in hope. To take the central word first. He
goes out in love, because he is the messenger
of the King of Love, and the message he bears
is the love message of God. The love of God is
shed abroad in his heart. The love of Christ
constraineth him. Therefore he loves those to
whom he is sent, and that in spite of all their
unworthiness, their defilement, their folly; for
this is the Love of God, the Love of Christ.
He goes out in faith; that is faith in God, in his
message, and therefore in all those to whom he

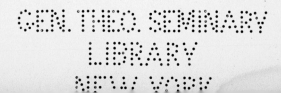

is sent.   As in the days of His flesh the faith
which the Son of God had in the sons of men
was the very inspiration of their faith in him,
so is it still with those who herald His Evangel.
And so he goes out in hope.   He knows nothing
of hopeless cases from the standpoint of the
power of his Gospel, and therefore his business
is to inspire hope in the most desponding and
dejected.

The Evangelist goes into all the world, that
is to the whole creation, groaning and travail-
ing together in pain; he faces its sorrow, its
sighing, and its sin, where they all originate, in
man; and his message is a royal proclamation of
Grace.   He publishes the good news that what
man cannot do for himself, or for the creation,
God in Christ has done; and that therefore
there is hope for man, and through him, as he
becomes in a new sense a son of God, for the
whole creation beneath him.

We may now consider the Evangel which is
thus to be proclaimed.   That Gospel is contained in the first four books of the New Testament.   It is not without significance that the
Church has named the writers Evangelists.
Two of them were Apostles, and two of them
were closely associated with the Apostles in

their service. Yet the nature of their apostolic writings constituted them Evangelists in very deed, for the story they tell is that of Jesus of Nazareth, the Son of God, and the Saviour of the world. That story is the Gospel.

In Paul's final summary of instructions to Timothy, we find a paragraph bounded by two injunctions; " Preach the Word "; and " Do the work of an Evangelist, fulfil thy ministry " (2 Tim. iv. 2–5). Again therefore the Word is the Gospel. The Evangelist is doing his work, not when he is telling anecdotes,—though these may be of great value when they are true and subservient; he is doing his work when he is telling the One Story of Jesus. This marks the limitation of his message. The limitation does not mean that his message is narrow or superficial. It is as broad as the love of God, and as profound as humanity's deepest spiritual needs. In the preaching of the Word by the Evangelist, the emphasis is on the message of God to men, as it meets their first needs, which are fundamental. The Evangel is God's love message to men. The whole of it is nowhere more perfectly summarized than in those most familiar, but most sublime words; " God so loved the world that He gave His only begotten

Son, that whosoever believeth on Him should
not perish, but have eternal life." That is the
Gospel. If that is a perfect summary, we may
find perhaps the most perfect analysis of content
in the words of our Lord concerning the mission of the Spirit in the world, spoken to His
disciples in the course of the paschal discourses
(John xvi. 8–11). We will confine ourselves
then to that passage, endeavouring to understand its main teaching.

Let us first observe the subjects with which
the Spirit deals in His ministry in the world;
" He . . . will convict the world in respect
of sin, and of righteousness, and of judgment."

These are the fundamental things of human
consciousness, when the soul is spiritually awakened. That awakening may come in a thousand ways; it may come over and over again,
without producing any effect whatever upon
life. But whenever it comes, these are the matters of which the soul is conscious, sin, righteousness, judgment.

Sin is first a volitional spiritual act; and then
it is an experience resulting from the act. The
spiritual act is that of disobedience. The experience resulting is that of ruin. To say that
sin is disobedience implies two things. Of these

the first is that of the relation of God to man; that He is Sovereign, and that His law is the true standard of human life. The second is that of man's relation to God; that he is capable of obedience to the law of God, and consequently that he is responsible. Sin fundamentally then is the wilful act of disobedience on the part of man, to the law of the Sovereign Lord to Whom man owes allegiance.

The resulting experience of ruin is that of the alienation of the soul from God. This issues in suffering, and in paralysis, both individually and socially. Man out of fellowship with God has lost the secret of joy, and of power; and so is unable to realize his life personally and relatively. The soul of man spiritually awakened, comes to this consciousness.

Righteousness is first a volitional spiritual attitude; and then it is an experience resulting from that attitude. The spiritual attitude is that of obedience. The experience resulting is that of realization. To say that righteousness is obedience, implies exactly the same things as to say that sin is disobedience; those namely, first of the Sovereignty of God, and secondly of the capacity and responsibility of man. Righteousness fundamentally then, is the will-

ing attitude of obedience on the part of man to
the good and acceptable and perfect will of God.

The resulting experience of realization is that
of the fellowship of the soul with God. This
issues in peace and joy, by the Holy Spirit's
enablement, both individually and socially.
Man in fellowship with God possesses the secret
of joy and of power; and so is able to realize his
life personally and relatively. The soul of man,
spiritually awakened, comes to this consciousness. It is involved in that of sin. Sin is the
consciousness of failure. Righteousness is the
consciousness of the ideal.

Judgment is government, executive action,
administration on the part of God. It is that
activity whereby He realizes His purposes, establishes and maintains order. It marks therefore the centre of human responsibility. Righteousness in human life is right relationship with
that judgment. Sin is rebellion against it, which
nevertheless cannot escape from its activity.
Judgment then in the case of man is that activity of God, wherein He rewards the righteous,
and punishes the wicked. The soul of man
spiritually awakened comes to this consciousness. It knows that judgment is active.

These then, the fundamental things of human

consciousness spiritually awakened, are the things concerning which the Spirit of God has a message, which message He delivers through those called to be Evangelists. That message is the Gospel. The Gospel is the Word of the Cross. The Word of the Cross is infinitely more than the story of the crucifixion. It is first the story of the Word made flesh; the presentation of the Person of Christ. It is then the story of the work of Christ; which includes the Cross, the resurrection, and the ascension. It is finally the story of the claim of Christ; the declaration of the appeal which the Word of the Cross makes to all those who hear it.

The Gospel first presents the Person of Christ. He is God manifest, in His character, in His law, in His activity. He is also Man unveiled, in His capacity, in His obedience, in His realization. So also therefore He is the One Whose presence in human history has unmasked evil, as the opposite of all that is in God, and the secret of human undoing. All this is the first part of the Gospel, the light in which man discovers the truth.

The heart of the Gospel is the story of the work of Christ, and of how He brings sin, righteousness, and judgment into relationship with Himself. Returning to our passage we find His declaration, to which we need to pay close attention.

"Of sin, because they believe not on Me." In these words our Lord made His superlative claim to perfect Saviourhood. By using them, He claimed to have provided perfect salvation for men. All the fact of sin He has dealt with. He is able to forgive, to cleanse, to restore. Sin now has a new meaning. It is the rejection of the Saviour. This Saviour is God the Sovereign Lord. To reject His grace then is the final and irremediable sin against His government. To yield to His grace is the central act of surrender to His government. It is the act that introduces the soul to the attitude of right relationship. That is the first note of the good news, which declares that "He died for our sins."

"Of righteousness, because I go to the Father; and ye behold Me no more." In these words our Lord made His superlative claim to absolute authority, and spiritual power. He not only died for our sins, He rose for our justification, and ascended to the right hand of the Father to receive gifts for men. Men, no longer beholding Him with the eyes of sense, may yet be brought into such living fellowship with Him, that in them may be fulfilled the ideal of righteousness. That is the second note of the Gospel.

"Of judgment, because the prince of this world hath been judged." In these words He made His superlative claim to complete victory. The Stronger than the strong has wrested the usurped sceptre from the enemy; and henceforth He exercises His executive authority, delivering those that are bound, and moving ever triumphantly forward towards the consummation, when He shall deliver up the perfected Kingdom to His Father. This is the final and triumphant note of the Gospel.

The Evangelist is called to declare that message, to herald that good news; and then to urge the claims of Christ. Those claims are threefold. He asks for confidence, for loyalty, for coöperation. Faith in Him is the condition of salvation; loyalty to Him the law of life; and coöperation with Him the activity of His own.

Thus then is revealed the Gospel of the Evangelist. It is the Word of God which proclaims His perfect provision in Christ for all human need. The gift is still bestowed and needed.

Ever and anon the Head of the Church has sent forth some Evangelist whose message has arrested the attention of the multitudes to such an extent that nations have been moved to their very depths. Such times have been wonderful times. We necessarily long and pray that they should be repeated. We need to be careful however lest such longing and prayer should make us neglectful of the work of perpetual evangelization, for the doing of which gifts are constantly bestowed. When God sends Francis, or Wesley, or Whitefield, or Jonathan Edwards, or Finney, or Moody and Sankey, let us rejoice, and coöperate with them; but in days when no conspicuous and outstanding personality is with us, let us recognize and help gladly all those, oftentimes simple and obscure souls, who know the joy of the Gospel, and are specially qualified to proclaim it in the ordinary ways of their more regular and quiet life. And moreover, let every man or woman who is possessed by this joy and power for evangelism exercise their gifts constantly and restfully.

If I may venture to quote a modern illustration of real success in evangelistic work, I shall refer to a man whom I have known intimately for over a generation. That man is Gipsy Smith. He is one of God's great gifts to His Church. I refer to him only to say that, under God, his success has been largely due to the fact that he has given himself wholly to evangelism. He has never attempted the work of Apostle, of Prophet, of Pastor and Teacher. But he has given himself with all devotion of mind and heart and will, both to the work of understanding the Gospel, and proclaiming it. His widespread popularity is accidental. He has never sought it. Had he done so he would not have had such conspicuous success.

Not every Evangelist is called to paths of service which result in popularity. Every Evangelist is called to devotion to his message and to its proclamation. Let the Evangelist magnify his office, as he glories in his Gospel.

D

THE WORD AS THE WISDOM OF THE PASTOR AND TEACHER

IN our preliminary chapter on "Ministry" we described Pastors and Teachers as: *Those who receive the obedient, and shepherd and instruct them.*

That definition properly links their work with that of Apostles, Prophets, and Evangelists. The apostolic teaching is that which the Pastor and Teacher interprets and applies to those who are brought into the fellowship of the Church. The work of the Prophet will inevitably result in the turning of those who hear and are influenced by the message, to the Church for instruction. To these the Pastor and Teacher will minister, as he sets forth the way of life more perfectly. This statement involves the truth that every living Church should be so organized that provision is made for those who are inquiring. Here the far-seeing wisdom of

John Wesley was manifested, in that his Society classes were formed for those who were so inquiring, as well as for those who had come to definite and conscious relationship with Christ. The work of the Evangelist, which is specifically that of proclaiming the Evangel, and bringing men into definite relationship with Christ, demands most especially the work of the Pastor and Teacher. Those who are new-born need care; and the work of shepherding and teaching them is that of the Pastor and Teacher. Thus we see that there is no conflict in the nature of the case between the different phases of this ministry of the Word. They are complementary. None is complete without the rest. Each is completed in the work of all.

This particular phase of the Ministry of the Word is defined by two words, Pastors and Teachers. These terms are mutually interpretive as we shall see. This is the only occasion of the occurrence of the particular word Pastor in the New Testament, either in the Authorized or Revised Versions. Elsewhere the Greek word is translated Shepherd. It has however passed into the currency of Church terms, and is valuable and suggestive. We shall follow the method of previous studies, and consider in turn; The Pastoral Gift; Function; and Wisdom.

In considering the Gift we turn first to the words themselves, that we may gather their first and simple suggestions.

Our word Pastor comes to us from the Latin *pastorem*, which means shepherd, and is derived from the verb to feed. The Greek word in the text, of which Pastor is a translation, is the word *pöimēn*, which is the word for shepherd, but the affinity of which is uncertain. It has been suggested by some that it is akin to *poīa*, herbage, grass; [1] and by others that it is derived from a root meaning to protect. Seeing that this question of affinity is uncertain, we may treat the word as a primitive one, and so employ it, according to its constant use, as referring to a shepherd, whose work it ever is to find pasturage and to protect.

The word Teacher is a translation of the Greek word *didaskalŏs*, which is clearly derived from *didaskō*, which is the causative form of the verb *daō*, to learn. Hence our word Teacher conveys the exact sense.

---

[1] Some render *poīa* in James iv. 14, "*Grass* is your life." Most agree however that *poīa* there is the feminine of *pöïŏs*, of what nature?

The use of the two words here to describe the one office is, as we have already said, of the nature of interpretation. On the purely natural level the word Pastor has to do with sheep, and the thoughts of feeding and protection are sufficient. When it is used of the flock of the Shepherd of souls, it needs the explanation of the word Teacher, which at once reveals the method of feeding and protection.

In our Lord's use of the figure of the Shepherd as applied to Himself (see John x.), the idea is radiantly set forth. The shepherd knows his sheep, and is known of the sheep. The shepherd takes oversight of his sheep; that is, he exercises rule over them, leading them out and in. The shepherd finds pasture for his sheep. The shepherd defends the sheep; if necessary, laying down his life that they may be preserved from the ravening wolf.

In our Lord's work as a Teacher we have the final interpretation of the method. It is that of imparting knowledge, carefully, patiently, progressively, and purposefully.

Thus the thought suggested by the double description is that of shepherding through teaching, and of teaching as a shepherd. The work of the shepherd is to be done by teaching.

The sheep are to be made to know the Chief Shepherd, to submit to His rule, to shelter within His defence, to avail themselves of His pasture, by careful, patient, progressive, purposeful instruction. The measure in which this can be done is the measure in which the Pastor is a Teacher,—himself taught in these very ways, and submitted to the teaching. The work of teaching is to be done in the spirit of the Shepherd. There must be concern to know the sheep, to exercise a true rule over them, to defend them at all costs, to provide their meat in due season. The measure in which this can be done is the measure in which the Teacher is a Pastor, so intimately in fellowship with the Shepherd heart of the Lord, as to be able to feed the lambs, to shepherd the sheep, to feed the sheep.

The place of the idea in the New Testament is assured. That of the Shepherd, as the figure of the true nature of rule and authority, is an Old Testament idea, but it is carried over into the New; and it is there that it finds its final interpretation in the Person and work of Christ Himself. Paul's employment of the word " Pastors " here is the only occasion where the word Shepherd is figuratively made use of in the New Testament for any other than Christ. Luke employs the word four times in the early part of his Gospel; not in a figurative sense, but definitely, of those who were keeping watch over their flocks by night in the neighbourhood of Bethlehem. Matthew, Mark, and John use it only of Christ. In describing the attitude of the Lord towards the multitudes which He saw as He went from place to place, teaching, preaching, healing, Matthew says that " He was moved with compassion for them, because they were distressed and scattered as sheep not having a shepherd." Clearly involved in that statement is the fact that He was the very Shepherd they needed. Our Lord according to John claimed to be " the Good Shepherd." The writer of the letter to the Hebrews called Him " that Great Shepherd." Peter wrote of Him as " the Chief Shepherd." All this makes the word " Pastors," as describing an office in the ministry of the Word, the more suggestive and sacred.

The word Teacher is also constantly employed in the Gospels of Christ Himself; and in the days of His flesh it was used of Him by foe and friend. His work of teaching is perpetually referred to, and in the passage in

Matthew previously quoted, it is stated that it
was as He went about *teaching*, that His compassion was moved for the multitudes. The
truths He uttered were persistently described
as His Teaching. When we come into the
Epistles we find this idea of teaching is constantly present in any consideration of the work
of the ministry. In the passage referred to in
an earlier consideration, where Paul was dealing
with the spiritual unity and organization of the
Christian Church, he used the word "Teachers"
alone, to describe the third order of those whom
God has set in the Church to fulfil its ministry.
It is of the utmost importance as we pass on to
consider the function of Pastors and Teachers,
that these two ideas should very clearly remain
with us, as revealing the method and manner of
the work. It is that of the oversight and instruction of the members of the flock.

In considering the pastoral function, we may
change the figure and employ a common one in
the New Testament writings, that of edification.
The work of Pastors and Teachers is that of edification. In this word there are special values in
the interpretation of this subject. It comes to us
from the Latin words, *aedis*, a building, and
ficāre, to make. Thus it exactly coincides with

the Greek word, which is composed of two words, *ŏikŏs*, a house, and *dĕmō*, to build. The idea of edification then is simply that of constructing a building, with appropriate materials. This larger conception is always included. Whatever is done with the material, is done in the interest of the whole building. In the house of God, every individual must be perfected in order to the perfecting of the whole. Those attracted by the Prophet, or enrolled by the Evangelist, constitute raw material. The work of the Pastor and Teacher is that of building them up into the Head, which is Christ, and so into the Body, which is the Church. Granted a group of persons who have heard, believed, obeyed, been born again; by the act of the Holy Spirit they are already members of the Christ, and so members of the Church; but their life is immature, their service is imperfect. To fall back upon the figure already used, they constitute raw material, the very material needed, but in the rough. They need much labour to fit them into their true place and function in the house of God. This is the work of the Pastor and Teacher. That work may at once be described as that of shepherding and teaching them, so that they come into complete subordination to Christ, and thus into perfect coördination in the Church.

This work is so supremely important that we will take time to look at it carefully in both these aspects, remembering their vital connection. Neither the one nor the other can be done separately. The perfecting of the individual is in order to the perfecting of the Church. The perfecting of the Church can only be accomplished by the perfecting of the individual.

The subordination of the individual soul to Christ demands three things; Christ must be apprehended intelligently, adored emotionally, and obeyed volitionally; and, as we shall see, that is the true order.

When considering the work of the Evangelist we spoke of the content of the Gospel as revealed in Christ's words in the paschal discourses. The Spirit's message is concerned with Sin, Righteousness, and Judgment, as these things,—fundamental in the consciousness of the spiritually awakened soul,—are dealt with by Christ. The vision of the Lord to which the soul yields itself in faith may be that of His sufficiency in all these matters. Or it may be that one aspect only is apprehended.   It may

be that He is first seen as the Saviour from sin.
It may be that His power to realize righteousness attracts the soul. It may be that the glory
of His government makes its appeal to the
heart. There is one Lord; and whatever aspect
of Truth appeals to the soul, there is one faith,
that of confidence in Him; which faith leads to
the one baptism in the Spirit, whereby the soul
receives the gift of life.

Now in every vision of Christ all Truth is im-
plicated; but the implicates are never immediately seen. This is a progressive experience,
and results from shepherding and teaching. In
order to perfect subordination, this intellectual
apprehension is necessary; and to lead the new-
born to it, is the sacred work of the Pastor and
Teacher. Without staying to dwell upon it
now, we may remind ourselves of the constantly
expressed desire of Paul, especially in his later
letters, that the children of God should have full
knowledge of Christ; and also of Peter's injunction that they should grow in the grace and
knowledge of our Lord and Saviour Jesus
Christ.

Such growing intellectual apprehension always results in deepening emotional adoration.
The more perfectly He is known, the more

amazed is the soul at the surpassing wonders of His grace and glory; and the deeper becomes its love, the more complete its adoration. If it be true as we sometimes sing that—

" Some have lost the love they had,"

then it is because they have for some reason failed to " follow on to know the Lord."

Such deepened love inevitably becomes the inspiration of more complete surrender to the will of the Lord, more perfect loyalty to all His service. "If a man love Me, he will keep My word," said the Lord Himself.

Thus it is evident that in order to the complete subordination of individual believers to the Lord, the matter of first importance is that they should know Him. To make Him known to them is the supreme business of the Teacher, and he must do his work as a Shepherd, knowing, ruling, defending, feeding. The whole conception of this individual responsibility is perfectly set forth by Paul in the words, " Admonishing every man, and teaching every man in all wisdom, that we may present every man perfect in Christ " (Col. i. 28).

These words breathe the true spirit and passion of the Pastor and Teacher. He is preeminently concerned about every individual soul. Observe the thrice repeated "every man." The Pastor-Teacher has far more to do than to preach to his congregation. That unquestionably he will do, and his preaching will be of the teaching order. But "every man" is never reached in general teaching. The Pastor-Teacher must in the necessity of the case acquaint himself with the individuals which make up his flock. He must get to know them personally. Every man has his own idiosyncrasy, peculiarity, problem, temptation, capacity. Therefore if every man is to be presented perfect in Christ, every man must be considered, prayed for in the light of that consideration, admonished and taught in wisdom in such ways as to meet his own particular need.

All this throws very clear and searching light on this subject of pastoral work, correcting much of modern irrelevancy therein. The true Pastor will do much more than make social calls upon members of his flock. That he will do. Indeed he will seek to mix with his people in all the interests of their lives, that he may know them, not inquisitorially, but sympathetically. But he will do all this, never forgetting that his particular work is that of perfecting them in

Christ, by admonishing them where necessary, and always by teaching them.

But again. All this must be done with a view to the bringing of the individual into coördination with the Church. It may be said that the work of perfecting every man in Christ is in itself that of bringing every man into coördination with the Church. While that is true, it is nevertheless of the utmost importance that this larger purpose should always be kept in mind. In this very connection Paul urged, as the first duty in a walk worthy of vocation, that we should give "diligence to keep the unity of the Spirit" (Eph. iv. 3).[1] This idea runs through his teaching on ministry in this epistle. The aim of ministry is that of "the building up of the body of Christ" (iv. 12); the purpose of all articulation within the body is that of "the increase of the body unto the building up of itself in love" (iv. 16); and the goal of everything is "the measure of the stature of the fulness of Christ" (iv. 13); which can only be realized in the whole Church. It is only as this is seen that the real importance of individual develop-

[1] The word he employed, and which we have translated *keep,* was *tĕrĕō,* to observe, that is, to keep in view; and not *phulassō,* to guard.

ment will be realized. The Pastor and Teacher then has to reveal to the souls under his care the purpose for which the Church exists; the consequent importance of her being a perfect organism; and the necessity therefore for the completeness of the individual member. In proportion as this is apprehended, the glory of the trivial, the responsibility of the small, the importance of the obscure, will be realized.

Perhaps there is nothing in which the Church has failed more conspicuously than in this realization of spiritual unity. It has sometimes been entirely lost sight of; and at others has been falsely apprehended. Yet it is at once the supreme glory of the Church, and its secret of power in its mission, that it is an organism, in which no member can fail, without in the measure of that failure wronging the Body, and preventing the true fulfilment of its function in the world. As one cog out of order in complex machinery stops the perfect action of the whole; as one link weak in a chain renders the whole chain weak; as one unguarded place in a fortress makes the whole citadel unsafe; so one member of the Church, failing to realize in vision and virtue its responsibility to the Church, halts the Church in its progress. The cog is for the machine, and its final perfection is that of its relation to the whole.   So with the link in the chain.   So with every part of the fortress.   So also each member of the Church, in life and service, is for the Church.   The work of the Pastor then, is ever that of coördinating every several member within the whole body of believers.

In all the ministry of the Word there is no more important work than that of the Pastor and Teacher, and none needing more consecration, zeal, and patience.   To fail here is to make abortive all apostolic, prophetic, and evangelistic labour.   It is with that conviction that we have taken longer in dealing with both gift and function than in the previous considerations; and also because in the natural order of things, in the history of the Church more have received this gift than either of the others.

The title selected for this Lecture is that of the Word as the Wisdom of the Pastor and Teacher.   Our reason for employing the word Wisdom in this connection is that of the apostolic use of it; especially Paul's teaching concerning it, in his first Corinthian letter; and his declaration already quoted from the Colossian letter that the responsibility of the ministry is that of " admonishing every man, and teaching every man in all wisdom." The word *sŏphia* was perfectly familiar in the apostolic age, and the people who read these writings had a very clear conception of what was intended by the term. Aristotle defined *sŏphia* as " mental excellence in its highest and fullest sense." Wisdom is broad and full intelligence; not as capacity merely, but as knowledge. Wisdom is in reality the sum total of Truth. It was in this sense that Paul used the word when writing to the Corinthians he said; " We speak wisdom among the perfect, yet a wisdom not of this age, nor of the rulers of this age which are coming to nought, but we speak God's wisdom in a mystery " (1 Cor. ii. 6). To this wisdom then he referred when he spoke of " Teaching every man in all wisdom." Immediately following this declaration we have a clear definition of this wisdom in which every man is to be taught in the words; " The mystery of God, even Christ, in Whom are all the treasures of wisdom and knowledge hidden " (Col. ii. 2, 3); and again later in his injunction, " Let the Word of Christ dwell in you richly in all wisdom " (Col. iii. 16).

The wisdom in which the Pastor and Teacher is to instruct the flock of God is that of the

Word of Christ; for in Him are all the treasures of wisdom and knowledge. To revert again to a phrase which was under consideration in a previous study, " As the truth is in Jesus "; the wisdom of the Christian Church is the sum total of Truth as that Truth has had its exposition in Jesus. The practical values of that wisdom are all suggested in the familiar words, " Christ Jesus, Who was made unto us Wisdom from God; both righteousness, and sanctification and redemption " (1 Cor. i. 30). I have intentionally adopted the marginal reading of the Revised Version here because I hold that " Wisdom from God " is the inclusive phrase, of which the practical analysis is given in the words " both righteousness and sanctification and redemption." Righteousness is that which is imputed to man when sin is put away; sanctification is the impartation to man of the life whereby righteousness is made the victorious principle of conduct; redemption is the final implanting of the likeness of Christ at His coming, whereby the judgment or government of Christ will come to its full and perfect victory. This then is the Wisdom which the Pastor and Teacher must impart; and these are the purposes for which it is to be taught.

That Wisdom is contained in the Sacred Writings, for in these alone we have the literature of the Christ. This is a most important fact. There is no Christian literature which is not the outcome of these New Testament writings, because only in these have we any history of Christ. By reference, and allusion, He is placed in human histories; but we know nothing from them of Who He was, of what He taught, of what He did. For all these we must come to the New Testament. To deny its accuracy is to be left without any certain knowledge concerning Him. All the spiritual and moral triumphs of two thousand years have been won by belief in the Christ, as He is presented in these writings. This matter however needs no argument here. We have the Truth about Christ in these writings in germ and in norm. It is there in germ. That is to say, that for its full understanding, there has been necessary the progressive interpretation of the Holy Spirit. The meaning of Christ, of His Person, of His teaching, of His work, was far profounder and more far reaching than the men who wrote the records knew. Indeed even to-day, " all the treasures of wisdom and knowledge " hidden in Him have not been discovered. There is certainly yet much more light and truth to break forth from " the Word of God."

But it must also be remembered that in these writings we have the truth concerning Christ in norm. That is to say that interpretation must be, in the nature of the case, exposition of the statements themselves; and not that of addition or denial. Every action of the mind in its attempt to grasp the meaning of the revelation must be guarded and corrected by the revelation. Directly an interpretation makes necessary the denial of a statement of the writings, it is thereby proved to be false. These things being granted, we say that the wisdom of the Pastor and Teacher is the Word of God in its totality, as it is contained in the Scriptures of Truth. It is his business, in the spirit of the true Shepherd, to understand, to explain, to apply, to enforce that Truth.

Thus as we conclude our consideration of the primitive Ideal we may draw attention to the fact that in every exercise of the Ministry of the Word, whether apostolic, prophetic, evangelistic, or pastoral, the fourth phase of the Word is realized.

It is that of the interpretation of the Word, first in the preparation of the Records; and then in their progressive unfolding; and the insistent urging of their claims; so that in and through Christ, the Eternal Word, life may be brought into harmony with the will of God. For this, as surely as for all revelation, the Spirit of God Who alone knoweth the deep things of God, is needed; and He is the ever-willing Guide of all who, called to the Work, yield themselves to His illumination.

When that is said, it must be added, that the Spirit of God in interpretation, only acts through the painstaking toil of those who are called upon to interpret the Wisdom of perfection to those who are to be presented "perfect in Christ." Ruskin's words should be carefully considered by all called to this holy service; "The Word of God . . . cannot be made a present of to anybody in morocco binding." Or again, what he wrote of "man's best wisdom," is more than ever true of this Wisdom; "When you come to a good book you must ask yourself—Am I inclined to work as an Australian miner would? Are my pickaxes and shovels in good order, and am I in good trim myself, my sleeves well up to the elbow, and my breath good, and my temper?"

When the Pastor and Teacher treats his

work in that spirit of complete dedication, then the Holy Spirit of consecration will work with him, and in his case it will never be true that—

" The hungry sheep look up—and are not fed."

III

The Modern Application

A

THE CHANGED CONDITIONS

SO far our study has been Biblical in a very narrow sense. This use of the word narrow is not intended as an apology for what we have done. It is rather an acknowledgment. The narrowness has been intentional and vital. In this matter, as in all others, "Narrow is the gate, and straitened is the way, that leadeth unto life."

We have looked at the beginnings of the Christian ministry of the Word; the times of Jesus, the times of the Apostles. We have been dealing with the primitive Ideal. Sometimes there is a suspicion of contempt in our use of the word primitive. There is no justification for any such contempt. The word simply means first or earliest of its kind. Thus we have been concerned with the beginnings, the origins. We have been at the sources of the great rivers.

George Borrow in his *Wild Wales* tells how when he had ascended Plynlimmon to see the sources of the rivers Severn, Wye, and Rheidol, he said to his guide; " It is not only necessary for me to see the sources of the rivers, but to drink of them, in order that in after times I may be able to harangue about them with a tone of confidence, and authority." This quaint conceit of the erratic genius has very definite value when applied to our studies. We have—as I said—been at the sources of the great rivers, and I trust we have been doing more than look at them; we have been drinking of them.

The springs among the glorious hills of Wales, however, are only known in all their glory, beauty, and strength in the resulting rivers; and ultimately in their return to that great sea, from which they first came through the ministry of clouds and mists, all sun-created. So also for us, the interpretation of these first things must finally be sought in all the growth and glory of the resulting rivers of grace and power.

It is of the utmost importance therefore that we should remember the law of development. We have seen it already operating in the earliest times, as set forth in the apostolic references to ministry.   Nothing is more patent in the book of the Acts than its revelation of the operation of this law in the Christian enterprise.   In that book we clearly see that the early Church was entirely unhampered by anything in the nature of stereotyped policy or method.   Where the Spirit of the Lord is, there is liberty; and among other things, that certainly means liberty to adapt methods to changing conditions.

It is equally important however that we remember that development is not destruction. Rightly apprehended, evolution always means involution.   That is not true evolution which destroys the original intention, or subverts its order.   It is therefore most pertinent that we inquire how far the primitive Ideals are practicable in modern conditions.

In dealing with this subject I propose to make two statements, following each by a question. The first of these is that the conditions are changed.   The second is that the conditions are unchanged.   The question in each case may be expressed in the use of the one word;—How? Along these lines of consideration and inquiry, we may come to an understanding of our own times, and of our own responsibility.

In considering the subject of changed conditions we are of course confined to what we usually describe as civilization. There are still regions where the conditions are unchanged, places where civilization is no more advanced than was that in the midst of which Christ and His Apostles did their work; as there are also still places in which man is living in savagery and darkness. Our concern is with the conditions of modern civilization, as it has advanced from that of the times of Christ and the first preachers of the Word. We shall confine our inquiry to three matters, those namely of Philosophy, Science, and Government. It goes without saying that we can only glance at these matters in the most general way.

The study of Philosophy may be said to have begun nearly six centuries before Christ. Plato declared that Philosophy was the child of wonder, and that is at once a fair definition, and a perfect vindication. Men began to be discontented with traditional and mythical explanations of the nature and origin of things, and sought to discover the truth. It is not inaccurate to say that Philosophy was from the beginning an attempt to answer the very question which Pilate asked of Jesus, " What is truth? " It is not necessary for us, here and now, to attempt to trace the history of the efforts made to answer that inquiry, nor indeed would it be possible. It is a history full of fascination, the story of the most wonderful activity of man, far surpassing all his material inventions, and indeed, the inspiration of them in their higher achievements.

Beginning with questions growing out of the vision of things that appear, that is the physical and manifest facts, it proceeded to questions concerning the inward mysteries, the things which do not appear, save as material things are their expression. The great period of creative thinking ended with the death of Aristotle, about three hundred years before Christ. This was followed by nearly two thousand years of comparative barrenness. The first eight centuries of this period are usually described as the period of Greek-Roman Philosophy. It was far more practical than speculative. The chief movements were those of Epicureanism, Stoicism, and Neo-Platonism; of which the first two were mainly ethical, while the last was more distinctly religious.

Before Christ came, four main philosophies of life had been produced, the Platonic, the Aristotelian, the Epicurean, and the Stoic. Of these the first resulted in an ascetic ideal of ethics; the second, subordinating the individual, aimed at social realization; the third became selfish in its pursuit of personal pleasure to the forgetfulness of all relative obligations; while the last demanded a self-control that was in itself selfish, and became cold and callous.

In a thought atmosphere largely influenced by these ideas, Jesus and His Apostles exercised their ministry; only it must be remembered that it was a dead and barren season even in these matters. When Paul preached at Athens, he was not speaking to living and original thinkers, but to men who were discussing words, and the theories of dead thinkers. It was a time when the dead hand of a great past was resting upon human thought, and Philosophy was decadent indeed.

Science in our modern sense of the word was not then born. It was a department of Philosophy. Bacon was the father of modern Science, by his introduction of the inductive method, the application of the faculty of logic to the consideration of facts. In the days of Jesus and His Apostles, the Hebrews believed with all simplicity the revelation of their Scriptures concerning the relation of the world to

God, interpreting that revelation with more or less of accuracy, in the light of the thinking of the age in which they lived. That thinking was largely nebulous, and certainly far from accurate, as all modern investigation has proved. The conception of the universe was narrow, and the understanding of the earth, by comparison with that of to-day, childish and ignorant.

As to Government, it is sufficient to say that Christ lived during the period of the Pax Romana, the peace established among nations under the rule of Rome. In other words it was the time when the known world was bruised and beaten into quietness and submission, under the military despotism which had usurped all government, and claimed the authority of Deity for its Imperators. It was the period when humanity was ground under the relentless and iron heel of brute force. It had no true liberty. In its chains, it made roads, conducted commercial enterprises, and all unknowingly to itself, prepared for the new age which was about to dawn. It was nevertheless a period of utmost cruelty, in which the vast majority of human beings were in actual slavery, and those supposed to be ruling, were in turn coerced by those above them, until the Emperor was reached, and he lived in perpetual terror of the assassin's dagger, or the intriguer's poison. It was the day of triumphant despotism, and of incipient revolution.

Philosophy was in a state of futile discussion of the great thinking of the past, without a ray of new light, or a breath of true inspiration. Science lay inchoate in the womb of this moribund Philosophy, satisfied for the moment with inaccurate guessing upon the basis of imperfect thinking. Government had wrought itself out in utter godlessness to a cruel and destructive despotism.

Under these conditions, there went forth into the world, the Apostles, Prophets, Evangelists, and Pastors and Teachers of the Christian Church. Their methods we have considered; and the content of their message; the Apostles declared the Word, as Truth is in Jesus; the Prophets were burdened with the Word of God; the Evangelists heralded the great Evangel; the Pastors and Teachers gathered the souls won from the prevailing darkness and death, and shepherded and instructed them in the Wisdom of God. With what speedy and far reaching victory they prosecuted their ministry we know. But the conditions are marvellously changed;

more largely as the result of their work than we sometimes recognize. Let us consider the change.

First as to Philosophy. Dr. Elias Compton, Professor of Philosophy in Wooster College, has said that "Apart from Christ, the western world has brought forth no other great Philosophy of life than the four—the Platonic, the Aristotelian, the Epicurean, and the Stoic. The modern systems are variants of these, with graftings from Christianity." This is a daring statement, but there is no doubt whatever that it is literally true. Any careful student of these philosophies of the past will discover how all that was excellent in them is included within the scope of Christian Truth, purged from alloy, and welded into the complete whole, of which Christ was in His personality the Incarnation, and in His ethic the Exponent. The long barren period in human Philosophy continued from the death of Aristotle in 322 B. C. to the time of Bacon and Descartes in the seventeenth century of the Christian era. It was not wholly barren, for Christian teaching was at work, and preparing for the modern period of activity which began three hundred years ago. After the strictly apostolic period came the patristic, with its discussion of the apostolic.   This was followed by that of the scholastic, which for a thousand years was active.

Then came the period when Bacon initiated the era of Science; and, under Descartes, Philosophy was born again, and entered upon its second period of activity.   The march of philosophic thought during these three hundred years may be indicated by the names of those men whose philosophies have contributed something to the sum total of human intelligence, and then passed, as others have succeeded them with yet more light.   Descartes, Hobbes, Spinoza, and Leibnitz led the way, as pure rationalists, declining to believe anything but those things which they considered axiomatic, that is, which could not be called in question.   Then came the period of the Empiricists, Locke, Berkeley, Hume, declining to receive anything as true that did not find ratification in known experience.   Closely allied with these was Kant the critic, yet his influence created a period in itself, by his insistence on pure, or *a priori* truths, and finally on the corner-stone of moral reason, conscience.   Then followed the great period of German idealism, of which the exponents were Fichte, Schelling, Schopenhauer, and the last and greatest, Hegel. Comte followed Hegel with Positivism, declaring that knowledge can only be of facts and their interrelations, thus swinging back towards the empiricism of Hume. Lotze took thinking back into the realm of idealism, as he declared that at last the universe must be interpreted in the terms of the spiritual. Most recently we have had the Pragmatic Philosophy of James and Dewey, which declares that the only way to know is to test by experience.

Thus it will be seen that since the days of Christ and His Apostles, and, as we have claimed, largely under their influence, directly or indirectly, Philosophy has gone far, but it has arrived at no final findings. It is still in a state of flux.

As to Science, we need only say that, during the three hundred years in which it has really been a separate section of human thought, it has made marvellous strides, and given to men the consciousness of a far more wonderful and much vaster universe.

Science and Philosophy for a generation have been enormously under the influence of the evolutionary theory, which has been applied backward to the beginnings of things, and forward to the inclusion of the ultimate realization of destiny. That there is an evolutionary process at work in the universe is universally admitted. That it accounts for everything is not only open to grave doubt, it is explicitly denied by Divine revelation. Nevertheless, modern conditions are dominated to a large extent by the theory.

When we come to Government we find an equally remarkable change in conditions. Notwithstanding the backward plunge of the last generation, culminating in the tragedy of the world war, to the attempt to master the world by brute force, we realize how far men have travelled towards the realization of the supremacy of the authority of ideas, and these of the highest,—Truth, Justice, Compassion. Moreover, to-day men are realizing the importance of freedom for all, rather than for the few; with its inevitable corollary of necessary bondage to the principles of Truth, Justice, and Compassion for all, in order to the freedom of all. It is well to remind ourselves that these higher things have been quite as clearly manifest in this world war as have been the lower. It is for these that millions went forth to suffer, and multitudes of them to die. Here the Christian influence has been direct and immediate. All these higher conceptions are the direct outcome of Christian Truth.

So far as the attempt to impose brute force upon humanity as the basis of government can be defeated by force of arms, it has been defeated upon these fields of blood and agony. That which succeeded two millenniums ago under Rome, has been crushed in its most recent adventure. The victory has been gained as the result of the power of the conceptions which came into human thinking with the coming of the Incarnate Word, and were proclaimed by the first ministers of that Word.

The victory is not yet complete. The battle passes finally into the realm of ideas, and their application to the actualities of life. There, it is now proceeding. Such is the full meaning of all our discussions in the realm of reconstruction. If brute force be dispossessed of the sceptre, into whose hand is it to pass, is the question of questions. If the disorderly impulses of men are not to be controlled ultimately by the mailed fist, how are they to be controlled? These are the problems creating the conditions under which the ministry of the Word is now to be exercised.

The preacher of to-day then has to face an

age of greater enlightenment, fuller knowledge, and higher conceptions of life, all largely resulting from the preaching of the Word according to the primitive Ideal; but he has still to face a world waiting for a true and perfect authority in order to the realization of perfect order.

We turn then to our second contention, which is that the conditions are unchanged. Here I begin with a general affirmation. It is Biblical, but it is borne out by all experience, and it is that humanity is essentially one, and in that sense it is unchanged. It is one in all the centuries; in all its own divisions of race, caste, and creed; in spite of its varied and ever-varying customs, habits, manners. That essential unity is that of its spiritual nature; it is not uniformity of bodily powers; it is not unanimity of mental conceptions; it is unity of spiritual being.

Of that unity there ever have been, and still are, two universal expressions, those namely of the quest for truth, and the sense of sin. These may be described by other phrases, but they are found in all human beings, call them by what names we may.

The quest for truth is the inspiration of education in a child, in an adult, in a race. It is simple, elemental, fundamental. In a child it expresses itself in the eternal Why? How? What? It is the desire to know. Call it inquisitiveness, curiosity, or what you will, it is there; persistently making demands, refusing to be silenced. It is everlastingly asking questions, seeking to discover secrets, knocking at barred doors. It persists in adult life, and all advance in thought and power results from the insistent determination to find out hidden things.

This ineradicable passion of humanity expresses itself in revolt, and in investigation. It revolts against custom, and against tradition. It breaks through the former, and violates the latter, in its determination to find the reason for each; and if there be no sufficient reason, then to find its way out into the larger spaces, the more ample freedom. It declines bondage, save as bondage can be proven to be the condition of freedom. Therefore it challenges all sanctions, demanding that they vindicate themselves in the terms of truth, which are the only terms of ultimate necessity. No Philosophy, no Science, no Religion, which refuses to yield to the asking, the seeking, the knocking of the human soul, is ultimately tolerated.

That universal spirit of man will consider the

suggestion, examine the hypothesis, attend to the claim, until it is halted and forbidden to inquire. When that is done, the soul refuses to submit, and flings over the barrier as an impertinence and an enemy. All this is the push of the human soul towards the facts, and that ultimately, if we know how to direct it, is the push of the human soul towards God. The activity of the soul is that of investigation, in the conduct of which it is often apparently ruthless; but the soul is never in such dire peril as when the process ceases, and it becomes content not to know, ceases its asking, abandons its seeking, no longer knocks.

It may be said that this cessation of effort is the normal condition of humanity. I can only reply that I do not believe it. It may be, and alas it is so, that men follow false lights, and seek to discover by wrong and disastrous methods, but deep down in the spiritual nature of man this quest is powerful and persistent.

It must be added however that the quest for truth is not in itself the finding of the Truth. Every discovery creates new problems, more complex than those which have been solved by investigation. Beyond the reach of the finite mind are vast spaces, which cannot be discov-

ered, and entrance to which can only come by
revelation, the yielding up of secrets as from
within. They are only yielded in answer to
investigation along true lines; but even then,
they must be given from within, or they will
never be found. The more earnest and sincere
the search for truth is, the more teachable becomes the soul. When the soul is not teachable, it is because it has ceased investigation.
It has stopped at some half-way house, which
perchance it may call agnosticism. Content-
ment with ignorance, that is with agnosticism,
is the paralysis of the spirit. Yet even when
man has so halted, the capacity remains. Can
these bones live? may be our question as we
look at men; but the answer of the Bible, and
the answer of experience is that by the breath
of the Lord they can. This is one phase of the
unchanged and unchanging fact in human con-
·ditions.

To leave the statement there, would be to
have recognized a fact, but not to have realized
the whole fact. Side by side with the quest for
truth, there is the sense of sin. Again I say
we may describe this by any other phrase. The
fact remains. It is that of humanity's abiding
bondage, its persistent paralysis. Men desiring

truth yield to a lie; endeavouring after goodness, they are unequal to realization. This
sense has many, and oftentimes strange, methods of expression. Sometimes it expresses itself by vehement denial. Such denial only
holds good when it operates in the realm of
theory, and of formulated terminology. A man
will deny sin, but will admit deflection from
strict veracity, departure from the mastery of
the highest; or at least he will confess that he
has not been able to realize perfectly his own
ideal of human life. He may try to console
himself by saying that no one has realized the
ideal, but that does not change the true nature
of his admission. Sometimes the sense of sin
is expressed in attempts to excuse it. This may
be done by laying the blame of it on others—a
very old human expedient; or by declaring
it to be a necessary part of the process of development, a more modern method. Such excuses
do not get rid of the fact. Far oftener than we
sometimes imagine, the sense of sin is expressed
within the soul in a poignant agony, born of the
consciousness of pollution, and of consequent incapacity. Whatever the expression, the fact
remains that Paul gave utterance to a great
elemental human consciousness when he wrote,

"When I would do good, evil is present with me."

It may be that the fact is laughed away; it may be tolerated as inevitable; it may be that it is the cause of perpetual agony; it is there, a persistent consciousness of humanity, in all ages, under all conditions, in spite of all human attempts to deal with it.

What effect have the changes we considered had upon these unchanged things of human experience? All the increased light in which we live, philosophical, scientific, and governmental, has but served to reveal our ignorance more profoundly.

Philosophy has not given us the final secret, Science has not solved the riddle of the universe. Men are still as far as ever, in their unaided wisdom, from the knowledge that brings rest because it illumines the mind, and gives rest in the midst of unsolved problems. Indeed it is questionable whether there ever was such unrest in the realm of human thought as there is to-day. Men are filled with a deadlier hopelessness, because they are less ignorant than they were, because access of knowledge has only meant the discovery of vaster mysteries than man had ever imagined.

The clearer light in human government, individual, social, national, has but served to make man more terrifically conscious of the awful power of sin, and the appalling corruption of human life. The things that are changed are after all the accidentals of life. The essentials are unchanged, and we are at once reminded that the primitive Ideal of preaching was fundamentally that it had to do with these essential things. It may be said with confidence that our Lord and His Apostles, Prophets, Evangelists, did not profess to deal with Philosophy, Science, or Government. All were included in their message; all have been affected by their ministry; but they dealt directly, invariably, with these very essential things of the soul. They went out to answer its quest for truth by the revelation of the God of Truth; and to deal with the sense of sin by proclaiming the Evangel of the way of deliverance. To deal with essentials is to control accidentals; and this was the aim of the primitive Ideal in the Ministry of the Word.

Nothing is more self-evident in any consideration of the history of the Christian ministry of the Word than the effect it has produced upon human conditions. It has flung light upon the whole realm of philosophical inquiry, introducing new elements, which it has been impossible for philosophers to ignore, and which have ensured an advance in human intelligence which is one of the most wonderful things in human history. It has claimed for men that freedom for investigation which has been the secret of all scientific activity and discovery. It has touched the human spirit with that sense of its own inherent greatness, which has resulted in its protest against every form of tyranny which holds men in bondage.

Thus the ministry of the Word has to be exercised to-day in changed conditions, which are the results of that same ministry, as it began with the Christ, was carried on by the earliest Apostles, Prophets, Evangelists, Pastors and Teachers; and has been maintained, with varying force and effectiveness, by the long and gracious succession of those called to the sacred work until now.

B

THE UNCHANGED OBLIGATION

I N this study we return to the more strictly
Biblical position, that is, to the Christian.
Recognizing the persistence in human experience of the quest for Truth, and of the sense
of sin, we face the subject of obligation.

If these facts of experience abide, and we
need not argue this further; and if the deposit
of the Christian Church be that Word of God
which meets these facts of experience, and that
is the assumption on which Christian Ministry
is based; then the fact of obligation is patent.
Our final obligation is that of preaching the
Word. To the consideration of that matter I
propose to lead up, by a brief discussion of the
wider human obligations which make that
preaching necessary.

Of these the fundamental is that man be right
with God. That, to the Christian, is the inclusive philosophy of life. It is based on two

matters which constitute the first and simplest things of our belief; those namely of the nature of man, and of the character of God.

The Biblical doctrine of man is that he is the creation of God; that his creation was a separate act, by which—although related to everything beneath him in the earthly scale of being—he was placed at an infinite distance from these lower forms, and given the right and the power to reign over them as the representative to them of the God from Whom all had come; that the nature of this act was that of an inbreathing of the breath of lives, whereby man became offspring of God, in the Divine image and likeness.

This conception of man necessarily involves the conviction that in the deepest fact of his personality, which is spiritual, he has in his very nature the closest relationship with God; a relationship which must be maintained if man is to realize his own life, fulfil his destiny, become experimentally what he is potentially. This necessity abides, in whatever condition man may find himself. Nothing can possibly be substituted in the spirit-life of man, for its direct access to God, and dealing with Him, without disaster of the most complete kind eventuating in the experience of man. Moreover, wherever that disaster has eventuated, nothing can set it right but the return of man to this relationship with God, which he has lost. All this, as we have said, is not based upon a law imposed upon man apart from the facts of his nature; it is inherent in his nature. To be alienated from the life of God is to be destroyed.

The Biblical doctrine as to the nature of God is that He is love. That is the final and inclusive truth. While that is the final revelation of the Bible concerning God, we need the Biblical interpretation of love, or else we may wander very wide of the mark in our exposition of this truth. God is holy and just, as surely as He is merciful and full of compassion. All these things are so because He is love. All this being so, the fact that man's first obligation is that of right relationship with Him is still more patent. To be right with Him is indeed to be conformed to His likeness, to share His nature; it is to be love, and such love as is holy and just, merciful and full of compassion. These are the things that make personal life really strong and beautiful, and apart from which human fellowship can never be brought to perfection of realization.

In his Gifford Lectures on " The Varieties of

Religious Experience," Professor James gave his final conclusion in these words:

"We and God have business with each other; and in opening ourselves to His influence our deepest destiny is fulfilled."

That conclusion of the modern philosopher is the starting point of Christian belief, the fact revealed in the first pages of the Bible.

The fundamental obligation resting upon the Christian ministry of the Word then is that of bringing men to the sense of this fact, and to willingness to yield to it. That which became almost the catch-word of a recent evangelistic movement, and which was resented by some, and sneered at by others, "Get right with God," was really the brief statement of the profoundest secret of human life.

Of this matter there are individual and social applications. Being right with God, means the realization of all the essential capacities of personality. For a moment leaving out of view the question of sin altogether, we say that a human being living in true relation with God is one in whom no natural power is atrophied, no natural capacity abortive, no natural purpose unfulfilled. It is a little difficult to think of this matter thus in the realm of the ideal, because we have no knowledge of what the conditions would be if there had been no failure. The only hint we have of this is the one of primitive conditions in a garden. There however the man failed. The only Man Who thus lived His life in right relationship from first to last was the Man Who lived that life in the imperfect conditions, resulting from sin. Had the first Adam lived spiritually as did the last Adam, every power of his own being realized and governed by the perfect will of God, all beneath him would have been perfected in being and use, through the sacred and delightful putting forth of his energy in work in fellowship with God. That is the golden goal, the far-off Divine event, to which the whole creation moves, as it sweeps round the cycles of the age of God. To-day it is for every man to remember that being right with God means that. The last Adam, our Lord and Saviour, realized it to perfection in His own personal life. There were limitations, self-emptyings, imposed upon Him in His humanity, as the result of His living in a ruined world; but, so far as was possible within those conditions, His human life was full, rich, perfect.

In thinking of men to-day, it is necessary to speak of *becoming* right with God, before we can speak of *being* right with Him.   Moreover there are senses in which that becoming will continue through life's pilgrimage.   Becoming right with God then, means the realization of our capacities in spite of sin.   This for men to-day is the fundamental personal obligation; but it is also the final impossibility, apart from the activity of the Divine Grace, whereby a man is born again, and thus enabled to come at last to the realization of his personality, in right relationship with God.

In all such consideration, God's racial purpose must not be lost sight of.   In the Divine purpose, humanity is not an aggregate of persons, living separate and independent lives.   It is a family, a fellowship, through which He will accomplish ends, which we may not yet see or know, but which are certainly far wider than this earth, and more extensive than that of which we speak as time.   The fundamental obligation upon which the minister of the Word has to insist, and to the realization of which he has to point the way, includes the regulation of human life in its inter-relationships.   This begins with the family circle, and stretches out through all the widening circles, until the whole race is included in its influence. This is at once the first ideal to be remembered, and the final result to be achieved.

This brings us to the second phase of obligation, which we may describe as the processionary, that is the obligation which is concerned with the processes by which the Divine purpose of bringing humanity into right relationship with Himself may be accomplished.

Inclusively we may say that it is, for this age, that of creating and conditioning a society, in which that rightness of relationship is realized and revealed. It will at once be seen that this is an exact description of the very purpose for which the Church of God exists in this world. The Church is the House of God, the Church of the living God, and as such, she is the pillar and ground of the Truth; that is, she is the instrument through which the light of truth shines upon the world. She is to be the example, and thus the witness, to the possibility of failing men being made right with God, and so of finding their way into right relationship among themselves.

Here also, necessarily, the obligation begins with the individual, and proceeds to the society. All the members of the society must be those who know God, and so are at perfect rest. They must be those who are in fellowship with God, and so are at ceaseless work. Therefore those who constitute the membership of the Society, the Church, the holy Nation, must be those who are redeemed from the pollution and paralysis of sin; and who share the life of God, through Him Who came to give men life, and that more abundantly.

Again, the mere gathering together of individuals, by the multiplying of the number of such, is not enough. These must be trained into all the experience of such submission to the one Lord, as shall result in the manifestation of the glorious liberty of the Kingdom of God.

This whole matter of the obligation as to the process is of the utmost importance, and cannot be overstated. The principle involved is that the Word of God can only be apprehended of men as it is incarnate. That is the reason of the Incarnation. It was only when the Word became flesh, and dwelt among men, that they beheld His glory, or came to a true apprehension of its message. It was when the Lord opened the understanding of His disciples after Pentecost, by showing the relation of their sacred Writings to Himself, that they understood the Scriptures. The value of the New Testament is that it creates a consciousness of Christ, which, flashing back upon the writings, illuminates them. The most powerful and prevailing exposition of these writings is never that of written or spoken interpretation. It is that of living witness. In proportion as the Christ of the New Testament is formed in individual souls, and manifested through the community sharing His life, is He able to carry forward the purpose of His heart, and lead other men into right relationship with God, and so to exhibit in human history the real glory of the Divine ideal for humanity. The strength of the Divine Society is the strength of the Divine Witness; and the strength of the Divine Witness is the process of the Divine Purpose and Work.

If the first obligation be that man be right with God; and the obligation as to processes be that a Society exist in which that rightness is realized and revealed; it follows that the ultimate obligation is concerned with the whole world. It may be expressed in the words of our Lord Himself in His intercessory prayer, when praying for the unity of His Church He

said, " That the world may believe," and " that
the world may know " (John xvii. 21, 23).

This is the unchanging purpose of God, and
it is a purpose which means the perfect meeting of the world's need, in and through man.
The word which our Lord employed in each
case was the inclusive word *kŏsmŏs*, showing
that while His work was preëminently on
behalf of man, it would operate through man
on behalf of the whole creation. That phrase
" the whole creation " is Paul's equivalent for
kŏsmŏs in the Roman letter, when he writes of
its groaning and waiting for the revealing of the
sons of God. It has been for the meeting of
this widest need that God has ever acted in His
Self-revelation, whether in the divers portions
spoken in times past through the prophets, or
through the final speech through the Son in
these days. Only as the world is kept in view,
and God's purpose is kept in mind, will the
Word of God in any form remain quick and
powerful. In this matter, no man and no community can long eat their morsel alone.

If we consider this world purpose a little
more fully as expressed in these simple and yet
sublime words of our Lord, we shall discover
how it exactly meets human need as we dis-

covered it when dealing with the unchanged
conditions.   Then we said that there persists in
human history and experience a twofold spiritual fact, which we described as, The Quest
for Truth, and The Sense of Sin.   Our Lord's
words indicate the Divine purpose in each of
these, but in the other order.   The sense of sin
is dealt with through belief; the quest for Truth
is answered through knowledge.   This is the
necessary order in human experience, for man
can only come into knowledge in its fulness, as
sin is put away.

The sense of sin is, as we have seen, a sense
of pollution and of paralysis.   The word of the
Gospel is a word that promises forgiveness and
life.   That in each case is a promise that is only
possible of belief if it comes from God.   When
the critics of our Lord said, " No man can forgive sins save God only," they said what was
perfectly true.   When our Lord claimed that
the gift of life must be a gift of God, He claimed
what none can dispute.   The question then for
man is as to whether He Who brought this message was sent by God.   To bring the world to
that belief is the ultimate purpose of God; for
by that faith men may have the sense of forgiveness, and the experience of life, full and

forceful. The only sin for which there is no forgiveness, and which is an age-abiding sin, is that of refusing to believe on Him Whom the Father hath sent. To this His words bear witness, " Of sin, because they believe not on Me."

The quest for Truth is a demand for knowledge. It is a revolt against all authority and limitation which are not final and inevitable. It is, as we said, in the last analysis, the push of the soul through towards God. The claim of Jesus to be the Truth was His claim that in Him man may find God. This claim we know He constantly made, and with such emphasis and clarity that there can be no mistaking of His meaning. The question for men then is as to whether He Who made this claim was really from God. To bring the world to that knowledge is the ultimate purpose of God; for in that knowledge men will find the answer to all their questions about the meaning of life, its origin, its development, its destiny. To know God as He is revealed in His Son is to have found the secret of all knowledge. The growth into it may be gradual, as it surely is, but there are no locked doors, no barred gates. From that knowledge, and in its light, man may go forward to perfected intellectual attainment.

To this also the words of our Lord bear witness; "This is life eternal, that they should know Thee, the only true God, and Him Whom Thou didst send, even Jesus Christ" (John xvii. 3).

Involved in all these matters is the fact that the immediate obligation of the Church is that the Word should be preached to these ends; in order that man may be set right with God; in order that the Society may be created through which the nature of this rightness may be revealed; and in order that the world may believe and know.

It is hardly necessary for me to enter into any lengthy argument in this series of studies as to the importance of preaching in itself, as a method of making the Word known. That has not been our theme at all. It has been assumed from first to last. Nevertheless it is so vital a matter that we may at least tarry with it for a brief space.

The whole subject is inclusively, and one may almost say exhaustively, dealt with in a passage in Paul's letter to the Romans (x. 13–15), in which man's dependence on preaching is stated absolutely; the method and value are revealed; and the one essential to success in preaching is

declared.   So important is the passage that we
will quote the whole of it:

> " Whosoever shall call upon the name of
> the Lord shall be saved.   How then shall
> they call on Him in Whom they have not
> believed?   And how shall they believe in
> Him Whom they have not heard?   And
> how shall they hear without a preacher?
> And how shall they preach except they be
> sent? "

In the opening affirmation the first necessity
of man is suggested, and the way in which it
is met is declared.   The necessity is that of
salvation.   This is the dealing with the sense
of sin and the quest for truth, which takes
man through forgiveness and life into knowledge.   The declaration is that men receive that
salvation when they call upon the name of the
Lord.

This affirmation is followed by four questions in sequence.   The first shows that men
will only call on the Lord as they believe in
Him.   Of course that qualifies the idea of calling on the name of the Lord, and shows that
it is much more than an intellectual, or formal
thing.   It is that calling of Jesus Lord, which
involves the surrender of the soul to Him, and

which, in his Corinthian letter, Paul said no
man could do but by the Holy Spirit.

The next question shows that men cannot
believe in some one whom, or of whom, they
have not heard.   It is interesting to observe in
passing that the Revisers, both English and
American, have rendered the question: "How
shall they believe in Him Whom they have not
heard?" instead of "How shall they believe in
Him of Whom they have not heard?" The
omission of the word "of" gives the idea a new
force, suggesting that it is necessary to *hear
Him,* and thus giving a special character to the
work of preaching.   In it, men must not only
hear about the Lord, they must hear Him.
Perhaps it is not safe to place too much
emphasis on this fact, but to me it does suggest
that preaching is only truly powerful when in
it the Lord Himself is made real to the hearer,
so that the Word is known as His own.

Then comes the question which reveals the
supreme importance of preaching, as it makes
hearing the Lord dependent upon a preacher.
The word for preacher and preaching here is
the word *kērussō,* which signifies the work of
the herald, the one who delivers the King's message with authority.

The final question recognizing the importance of preaching reveals the secret of success therein. It is that the preacher should be sent. The Christian preacher is called and sent by the fact that he is equipped for his work by his gift, of which we shall have more to say in our next study.

The value of this passage for us now is its revelation of the importance of preaching, and the light it throws on the immediate obligation of those in the Ministry of the Word.

The Word is to be proclaimed apostolically, as to its system, and balance and proportion; evangelistically, as to its glorious news, and the claim it makes upon men concerning their salvation; prophetically, as to its bearing upon all human affairs; and pastorally, as to its sustenance of life, and the consequent growth of the soul into Him Who is the Head, and so into its true place in the Church.

No change in the accidental conditions of human thought and circumstances has changed the essential facts of human nature. Therefore the obligation to preach the Word abides, and is as urgent as it ever was. To make men right with God; to edify the Christian Society; to reach the world with the Evangel, and to make it know the truth; these are the most important things of human life; and to do this work men are still given gifts by the Head of the Church, which it is at their peril they fail to employ.

The value of the written Word for this work is patent; as also is its perfect suitability. There are times when we are tempted to wish that we found more explicit instructions in the presence of problems; but a more careful consideration will show how much better is the Divine way than the human. If in the Sacred Writings we had merely detailed applications of the Word of God to any one age, they would inevitably become obsolete with the passing of that age. Instead we have the statement of eternal truths and principles with illustrative applications. These things abide, and have new application in every age. Thus to quote the words of our Lord; "Every scribe who hath been made a disciple to the Kingdom of Heaven is like unto a man that is a householder, which bringeth forth out of his treasure things new and old." To do this is the abiding obligation of every man called to the Ministry of the Word.

The realization of this obligation must surely

settle very many questions which inevitably arise in the exercise of that sacred ministry. All we have said about the changed conditions in the midst of which we have to preach the Word to-day, recognizes that we do so in the midst of constantly new problems, and ever varying situations.

The new vigour of philosophic inquiry is creating new attitudes of mind, and giving rise to new problems in every department of human knowledge. These are not merely interesting, they are of vital importance to human life. What then is the attitude of the preacher of the Word to be towards them? He must be conscious of them. They will confront him in all his reading, both the more serious, and the ephemeral. He knows that his people are reading the same things, and are being influenced by them. Is he to refuse to consider them? By no means. His first duty is to do everything that lies in his power to make himself familiar with them. In this sense he must keep abreast of his times. But he will not change his message in order to bring it into conformity with these changing and fluctuating currents of human opinion. He will however give himself with new diligence to the study of his message, in order that he may apprehend and proclaim its bearing upon these movements of the human mind.

In this process he need have no fear. The Word of God liveth and abideth for ever. It deals, not with the accidentals of thought, but with Truth essentially, and therefore has persistent and corrective bearing upon all human thought. The obligation of the minister of the Word is that of discovering and proclaiming that bearing. In the process he may have to change his mind, but never his message. That is to say he may discover that his apprehension of the message has been faulty. Then he must honestly and fearlessly say so. Consistency with yesterday's honest conviction may be of the essence of dishonesty. Loyalty to the authority of the Word in itself is of the essence of the obligation resting upon its minister.

So also the very restlessness of men in all matters social and economic is creating new situations. These also are of supreme importance to human well-being. Of these the preacher must, and ought, to be conscious. To live in ignorance of them is to be unable to bring to bear upon them the witness of the Word of God. That is his work. He is not called upon to join committees to discuss these situations, in order to help men to discover some solution of their own. He must be able to bring to bear upon their discussions the searchlight of the Divine Law, and the guidance of the Divine Will. That is his one obligation.

Again we say he need have no fear. No situation has arisen or can arise in human life, individual, social, or national, which is outside the Divine interest; and within the compass of the Truth as it is revealed in Christ, there is explanation and direction, accepting and following which, men will be led into the highest conditions of life. The obligation which abides is a grave one, but it is most gracious, for it has to do with the things for which the world is waiting, and without which it can find neither righteousness, peace, nor joy.

C

THE PREPARATION OF THE MINISTRY

WHEN dealing with the fundamental conception of the ministry, and again in our last study, I referred to the fact that in each case the gift bestowed by the Head of the Church is potentially the necessary qualification for the doing of the work. This we must now consider a little more particularly, because it is vital in the consideration of the subject of the training of ministers.

Training is for those who have received gifts. Apart from the gift, training can never prepare men for the Ministry of the Word. I often wish that our Protestant Churches, especially the Free Churches, had not lost the word *Vocation*, concerning the ministry; and that, in the sense in which it is employed in the Roman Church. Men cannot choose to become ministers of the Word. This calling is differentiated from all others, in this very fact. While, as we shall see presently, natural fitness is important,

176

it is not enough. While a man can, upon the ground of natural ability, decide whether he will be doctor, lawyer, or commercial man, he cannot so choose to become a minister. The words of our Lord are of abiding application, and must be taken in their fullest sense; "Ye have not chosen Me, but I have chosen you." So strongly do I feel upon this matter, that I never ask men to enter the Christian ministry. I have had occasion, in the exercise of the pastoral office, to ask some man who seemed to me to have special fitness for the work of the ministry, whether he had carefully considered what was his Lord's will for him in the matter. This, however, is quite a different thing from a general or particular appeal, which seems to suggest that men can choose the Ministry of the Word as a calling. The only men who can really enter this Ministry are those whom the Lord chooses, calls, and equips, by the bestowment of gifts according to the wisdom of His will.

In considering this initial subject of gifts, there are two elements which must be recognized; and which we may describe as the supernatural and the natural. I confess this is a distinction which ultimately I dislike, but it has its use, and we will employ the terms in the generally accepted sense.

For the work of the Ministry of the Word the gift which we thus describe as supernatural is supreme. This is the gift which is definitely bestowed upon a man by the Head of the Church through the Spirit; and which gives him the equipment he needs for the exercise of that ministry as an Apostle, a Prophet, an Evangelist, or a Pastor and Teacher.

In the Ephesian passage to which we have given attention in considering the different phases of the Ministry of the Word, we have the central declaration concerning this matter. From the passage let us take an extract, enabling us to see that declaration in all its simplicity;

" When He ascended on high, He led captivity captive, and gave gifts unto men. . . . And He gave some, apostles; and some, prophets; and some, evangelists; and some, pastors and teachers " (Eph. iv. 8 and 11).

That is the true sequence so far as this subject of gifts is concerned. In this statement the twice repeated verb " gave " (*didōmi*), and the noun " gifts " (*dōma*), are related, and refer to gifts in the simplest way, as a bestowment, the emphasis being upon the freedom of the gift. The word "gift" (*dōrĕa*) in a previous verse, "the measure of the gift of Christ" (ver. 7) also means a gratuity, but in use carries the thought of a sacrifice or offering. Now the whole context shows that these gifts for the exercise of the Ministry of the Word are freely bestowed by the Head of the Church, in virtue of His victorious ascension, to the place of full and final authority; an ascension made possible by His descent into the lower parts of the earth, and all He accomplished there. The gifts then are bestowed by infinite grace, and absolute authority.

There is, however, another New Testament word which we must consider if we are to apprehend the full value of these gifts. It is the word *charisma*. This is the word employed by Paul in his Corinthian letter when dealing with the same subject. He also used it in his Roman letter, and in writing to Timothy about the work of the ministry. Peter also used it once (1 Pet. iv. 10). This is the only occurrence of the word in the New Testament outside the writings of Paul. Thayer clearly sets forth what he calls "the technical Pauline sense" of the term in these words:

> "*Charismata* (gifts) denote extraordinary powers, distinguishing certain Christians, and enabling them to serve the Church of Christ, the reception of which is due to the power of Divine Grace operating in their souls by the Holy Spirit."

That definition of course applies to other gifts than those bestowed for the ministry of the Word, but it certainly includes them. Thus a gift is a bestowment of grace, which is an endowment, a qualification, a faculty. In the possession of such a gift a man is potentially prepared for the exercise of a function. Apart from its possession he cannot do the work for which it is the equipment.

The second element is that which we may describe as natural, although natural gifts are also supernatural in that they are Divinely implanted. Whatever special natural capacity or aptitude a man has, he possesses because God the Father of spirits gave it to him in his creation. These natural gifts always constitute the instruments of supernatural gifts in the economy of God.

The gift of the Apostle is bestowed upon men of very varied mental powers, but upon men who are supremely men of thought, capable of

analytic, synthetic approach to truth. Hence
the abiding value of the apostolic gift is that
Truth ever needs setting forth in proper balance and proportion; in every new age of human thinking, it demands the true terms of expression in order to accurate apprehension.
Here is the work of Translators and Theolo-
gians.

The gift of the Prophet is bestowed upon
men of naturally statesmanlike outlook, and of
clear powers of speech. Thus the constant
value of the prophetic gift is that Truth ever
demands application to all the new circumstances of human life as they arise.

The gift of the Evangelist is bestowed upon
men who naturally are possessed of the power
of speech and of persuasion. The persistent
value of the evangelistic gift is that under all
circumstances, and to all classes of men, the call
of the Gospel needs to have utterance.

The gift of the Pastor and Teacher is bestowed upon men who supremely have aptitude
for teaching, and are full of patience. The perpetual value of the pastoral and didactic gift is
that as men and women are brought into the
Christian experience, they need training and
guidance.

All this I hold most strongly. A great deal that has been said about a gift bestowed making a man a preacher who had no natural ability, is sheer nonsense. God's natural and spiritual worlds are not so out of joint. Nevertheless the final truth is that no natural ability qualifies a man for the work of the Ministry of the Word, apart from the bestowment of a gift of grace which is a spiritual qualification. There can be no training of the minister until that gift is received.

It may be well at once to say that the consciousness of the reception of a gift, that is of a call to the ministry, may come in many ways, and may vary in the most divers manners. To one man it comes suddenly, like the flash of the lightning, the peal of a trumpet. To others it comes slowly, like the dawn creeping over the hills, the whisper of a distant voice. To some it comes as a great joy, filling the soul with hope and ecstasy. To others it comes through travail, and is almost a sorrow and a pain. One is at once filled with the sense of confidence and strength; another trembles and shrinks, and is conscious only of appalling weakness.

These different experiences are natural, and are largely due to temperament. The spiritual fact is the certainty, from which no man can escape who has received the gift, and felt its sacred heat. Until men have the most profound conviction and certainty in this matter, no training of them should be attempted. It is here that the importance and value of the Church's recognition is first manifested. I do not think any Theological College or Seminary ought to receive a man for training whose personal sense of a call is not reinforced by the recognition and endorsement of the Church.

Necessarily this opens a wide subject, and one which it is not within the province of these lectures to deal with, that namely of the organism of the Christian Church, and its maintenance in full strength. Much of our modern Church life lacks the experience of fellowship to so large a degree—even when the theory is acknowledged—that it cannot exercise this function of coöperation in the work of setting men apart to the work of the ministry. The man who receives the Divine call may be comparatively, and indeed often completely, unknown to the majority of those who constitute the membership. It is impossible therefore for them to come to anything like spiritual conclusion on the subject. Moreover too often, even when the man is known, our modern methods of work, and the organizations connected therewith, afford no opportunity for our young men to exercise their gift under the sympathetic observation of the Church. Both these facts work disadvantageously—to put it no more strongly—in the interest of the ministry. Every local church, especially, should constitute a true fellowship, in which the life of the whole is strengthened by the knowledge of each, and contribution in prayer and converse is made by all to each, and by each to all. Every church should moreover have some training ground for its young people in Christian speech, and that, not relegated to a society separated from the main currents of its life, but nurtured in the very midst thereof.

All this being granted, we may now consider how those men who have received one of these gifts are to be trained. Neither the man himself, nor they who are responsible for his training may, at first, have any definite conviction as to the particular nature of the gift. That will emerge in the course of training, and should qualify the later stages especially. At times a man from the beginning is conscious of the peculiar gift with which he is entrusted. When

that is so, training should be from the beginning
with a view to its development. These particular applications however must be left. It is not
a difficult task. The nature of the gift suggests
the special treatment necessary for its cultivation in each case. I propose to deal with the
subject in the most general way.

There are four phases of training which must
be kept in mind, and I shall define them in general terms as, Academical, Theological, Practical, and Spiritual. Let me at once say that the
first two should be taken in the order named,
first the academical, and then the theological;
while the last two, the practical and spiritual,
should run concurrently through all the course.

The training which I have called academical
is really the training of the mind. It is that
which, in our present University system of education, we should describe as the Arts Course.
This should, in my view, be of the widest nature, and as thorough as possible. The value
of this is twofold. First, and again in my view,
principally, is the fact that such a course of
mental discipline trains and perfects the instrument. There is nothing more important than
that men should be taught to think for themselves, and to think their way through. Now I

affirm it as my strong conviction, that men do not do either the one or the other without serious discipline. In the realm of Christian preaching, it is as true as in any other, that evil is wrought by want of thought as well as want of heart. It must be remembered that the Word of God is no small matter. We may do incalculable harm by talking about the simple Gospel. There is a simplicity in the Gospel as there is in Christ, from which we do well that we do not depart. But it is not the simplicity of superficiality. There are the profoundest depths in the Truth, as there are in Him, in Whom it has pleased the Father that all the fullness of the Godhead should dwell corporeally; and we equally do well not to forget this fact. To deal with these matters, it is of the greatest value that the mind should in itself be perfectly trained, in order that in its approach to the Truth, it may do no bungling work. It is true that the Apostle is called upon to make Truth clear to others; the Prophet to make its application living; the Evangelist to make its first message simple; the Pastor and Teacher to make it available to the youngest and weakest disciple; but the more complete the knowledge of the preacher in each case, the more successful will he be in accomplishing this purpose. The completeness of the preacher's knowledge depends to a large extent on the perfecting of the instrument of his mind. Hence the first value of academic training.

The second value is that of the acquisition of knowledge in itself. Nothing is without some value in the work of preaching. The man who, in the finest sense of the word, is a well-read man, is thereby greatly enriched for the work of the ministry; and that for two reasons. First, because over the whole realm of knowledge Christ is King, and whatever department a man knows, is in itself a part of the territory over which His sway extends. Secondly, because in all realms of knowledge illustrations may be gathered which are of the utmost force in the elucidation and application of the Truth he has to proclaim. Of course the realm of knowledge is so vast that no one man in a lifetime can cover the whole of it; and men preparing for the ministry have a specific subject on which to specialize. Therefore selections must be made in the interest of the special work.

Generally speaking I should urge that the study of language should be kept to the front; especially those languages in which the Sacred

Scriptures were written. A careful and thorough study of English, the tongue in which preaching is to be done, is of the greatest importance. The poor Anglo-Saxon of some Hebrew and Greek scholars is deplorable.

Then all history is of enormous value. It is not without profound significance that the Hebrews included the Historic books in the class of Prophetic writings. They understood first, the truth about prophecy, that it is the speaking forth of the Word of the Lord supremely, and that the predictive element is only one part of it. Then, they realized that the true value of history is created by the fact that it reveals the way of the Divine government in the past, and so teaches men fundamental things concerning their present actions. This is as true of history outside the Biblical Literature as of that within, for as Paul said on Mars Hill, God " made of one every nation of men for to dwell on all the face of the earth, having determined their appointed seasons, and the bounds of their habitation." Hence the importance of this study.

The importance of the study of human systems of philosophy cannot be overestimated. This I need not stay to emphasize in view of what we have already said concerning it in a previous lecture.

The science of psychology is perhaps only yet in its infancy, but the infant is singularly well nourished, and full of strength, and as it seems to me, those called to the Ministry of the Word cannot afford to neglect it. I do not suggest that they are to be experts in the science, or that they will be called to lecture on it; but an understanding of the mind of man, so far as it is known, must be of untold value to those who have to deal with the Truth. It is unanimously conceded that such knowledge is important in educational work. It is not enough to know the subject to be taught. It is necessary to know the mind of those to be taught.

Personally, moreover, I would compel every man who is going to preach to take a course in the theory and practice of pedagogy, and of elocution. The value of knowing how to impart knowledge, which is of the very essence of real teaching, is fundamental to the work of proclaiming the Truth, and that in every phase of the work of the Ministry. A man may be able to write, and to recite a treatise, and such work is excellent; but it is of very much greater service to men and to the cause of Christ, if he be able so to impart the knowledge that others may receive it. It may be that preaching which is of this nature may lack something of literary finish, but I would sacrifice a good deal in the interests of clarity. Elocution in this regard is not to be neglected. Anything strained, artificial, theatrical, is to be sedulously avoided; but articulation, enunciation, light and shade, should be as sedulously cultivated.

For my illustrations I am prepared to apologize, but not for my main contention that the minister of the Word cannot know too much, nor have too thorough a training academically.

All this however is preliminary; and because it is preliminary my conviction is that it ought to be taken first in order of time. Wherever possible I would prevent any man approaching the study of Systematic Theology until his academic training was complete. It is my own conviction that to bring a half-trained mind, or a mind in process of training, to that study is a grave mistake, and issues in those hasty judgments which are too often mistaken for advanced thought. Necessarily throughout the whole of this academic training, the student will continue his reading and diligent study of the Scriptures themselves. This for devotional purposes, and also to give him the grounding in knowledge of them, which will be of value when he begins the more systematic study of Theology.

The mind having been thus trained in the academic course, the great work may begin, that namely of the instruction of the trained mind in its special subject, which we now define by the general term Theology. To that term I have no objection, providing always that we remember that it connotes more than it means philologically. Technically, Theology is the science of God, and that is the knowledge of God. According to our Lord Himself this is life eternal. It is therefore the Word of God in all its fulness.

With any particular method or system of Theology I have nothing whatever to do now, and I am not proposing to tarry here, save to insist upon one or two fundamental matters. The first is that of the absolute necessity for the training of every man who enters the ministry in Theology in this widest sense. Here a man must do more than specialize in a department. He must see the whole, so as to realize the value of the parts. Nothing is more dangerous than the over-emphasis of a truth. Every phase of Truth is not only completed by, it is corrected by, every other phase. George Herbert's words about the Bible may be quoted here as most appropriate to the subject of Theology;

" O that I knew how all thy lights combine,
　And the configurations of their glory!
Seeing not only how each verse doth shine,
　But all the constellations of the story."

There have been many systems of Theology. They are still emerging. Doubtless there will be many more. These are all valuable,—little systems, that have their day, and cease to be. They are valuable, both in their day, and in their ceasing to be; as they help men to immediate understanding, and then make way for new statements adapted to the new age. The one System that is for every successive day, and that does not cease to be, is that which we have in the Bible.

Fundamentally then theological training is Biblical, and to the Bible Literature itself most earnest attention must be given. It should have the supreme place in theological training. Let the method with all human systems be eclectic. The more of these a man can examine in his course the better, providing that he allows them to be tested by the Biblical standard, and does not attempt to crowd the Biblical system into their narrow formulæ. That is all I desire to say on that subject.

We now come to the two phases of training that should be conterminous with the whole course, those namely which are practical and spiritual.

From the beginning of their training, men called to the exercise of the ministry of the Word should have practice in preaching under wise and sympathetic oversight. It is well also if he can have pastoral practice, also under apostolic oversight. It may be objected that the plea I have urged for the academic course having the first period in training, is against this idea, because the student has no theological training. To that I should reply; first, that every man who is a Christian believer, and is conscious of the call to preach, has already some knowledge of the Word; and secondly, that neither the man himself nor his congregation will expect that his preaching should be other than the simple statement of those things which he believes. I think no greater mistake can be made than to neglect preaching for a number of years.

Here I propose to take the opportunity of protesting with all the force of the strongest conviction against the ordinary sermon-class, in which a man is called upon to preach before his fellow students and members of the faculty. The whole method cuts at the root of the true idea of preaching. The man prepares for his sermon-class, from an entirely wrong motive. His sermon will be criticized, sometimes kindly, sometimes brutally, from the lower standards of consideration. Its essential character of being a message of God to men cannot be dealt with in a sermon-class. It is above and beyond criticism. Moreover what man can preach *to* such an audience? Of course he does not attempt to do so. He preaches *before* them, and preaching before men is not preaching in the Biblical sense. No; this is not the practice for which I plead. Let these men in training be sent out two by two into the villages, into the towns, especially to difficult places; and let them go to preach the Truth as they know it, to the people. Let the two be encouraged to go in manly, sane, and yet distinctly spiritual fellowship; let them go to help each other, not to manifest their cleverness either in the preaching, or in the criticism. Then they will do two things at once. They will help those to whom they go, and they will grow in the ability to deal with men as they preach.

During the whole course of training, such preaching should be under the guidance of competent men, both as to its matter and its method. As to the matter, written sermons should be submitted, such sermons as have actually been preached, that the Teacher may show the faults of reasoning, or the failures of illustrations; or, on the other hand, encourage evident ability in certain directions, as it manifests itself. These men should be encouraged to preach from notes, and these notes should be submitted for the same kind of revision. As to the method, the Professor of Homiletics would gain much of real influence if in turn he was the other one of the two, and so heard the man himself preach. Let him walk home with the student, or get him into his study for a quiet talk afterwards, and point out the failures and excellencies which he observed. We have sadly neglected the true practical training of men for the work of preaching, and the neglect is being felt everywhere to-day.

The final matter is that of spiritual training. In some senses this is supreme. The first experience of the man knowing that he is called to the ministry of the Word, is inevitably that of the grandeur and solemnity of the work. He faces it with a sense of joy, mingled with fear and trembling.

The perils of the period of training are very definite. Inevitably the necessary work of critical investigation will seem to challenge everything that he has held most sacred. From this there can be no escape, and I am inclined to say that the man who does escape it, misses one of the surest methods to the finding of a firmer and larger faith. Nevertheless the process is a very searching one.

Then there is the special peril of the community of purpose and of faith. Christian men in other walks of life have the advantage of the friction caused by daily contact with those who are not Christians. Students for the ministry, for a period, largely lack this. Very often too, a sane dread of anything that savours of cant and unreality will prevent that spiritual intercourse which is really necessary to the development of strong spiritual life. There is also the peril of the first gaining of new knowledge. A man is always at least threatened with the vain imagination that he knows much, when really he has hardly found out how ignorant he is.

All these things, and many others peculiar to the period of training, can only be guarded against by the careful cultivation of the habits of the truly religious life. Habits I say, remembering that they have to be *formed*, as certainly as do evil habits. Theological students need pastoral oversight as surely as do other Christian people, and of a very special kind.

Happy are the men who, called to the Ministry, have the privilege of a full and careful training; and highly privileged are those to whom the sacred work is committed.

D

THE EXERCISE OF THE VOCATION

THE day when a man stands girded at the threshold of his actual work in the ministry of the Word, is a day full of mystic wonder. He is conscious of strange lights and shadows, of joy and of fear, of hope and almost of despair. The opportunities of service are seen to be at once so vast, and so full of solemnity, that he is seized with a sense of inability, and of unworthiness. He feels in his own soul what the Apostle undoubtedly felt as he inquired; "Who is sufficient for these things?" Nevertheless he is conscious anew of the fact that his call was from God, and that Divine resources are ever at the disposal of those called to Divine service; and so a sense of dependence is also a sense of confidence. These apparently conflicting emotions fill the soul with a great and reverent awe.

Perhaps the most common disaster in min-

isterial life is the loss of this very sense of awe.
The glory passes; the light becomes dim; the
wonder ceases; and work becomes routine, and
preaching a drudgery.   How is this to be obvi-
ated, and the first glory maintained undimmed?
This is really a great question, demanding serious consideration.   I propose to deal with it so
far as I am able strictly from the positive side.
There are four matters which seem to me to be
of paramount importance in the exercise of the
vocation of the ministry of the Word.   They
are; first, the prayerful culture of the spiritual
life; secondly, the persistent study of the Word;
thirdly, the practice of purposeful preaching;
and finally, the patient shepherding of the flock.

Wherever a man gives himself with all his
heart and mind and will to these things, the
glad surprise and mystic glory of his work will
never cease.   Dark days, and weary ways, he
will certainly know; but so also did his Lord.
Nevertheless the light for Him never failed, and
all the tiresome ways led onward to the glorious goal.   So also will it be with those whom
He calls, sends, accompanies, if they are true to
Him and to His service.   Of these things then
let us think.

The matter of first importance is that of the

culture of the spiritual life, or to put it in another way, the maintenance of life in the Spirit. The minister of the Word must ever remember that his one business is to deal with spiritual things. This by no means suggests that he is to separate spiritual truth and being from things mental and material, as though they were in some sense abstractions, having no living relation with these matters. But it is of absolute urgency in order to the exercise of his true function, that he should remember that he is not called and equipped by the heavenly gift for dealing with the mental and the material, apart from the spiritual. His one business in the realm of thought is to bring to bear upon it the light of the eternal Wisdom; and his one responsibility in the realm of action is to seek to inspire it with spiritual principle and passion. The work of the Christian preacher is that of bringing to bear upon human words, opinions, teachings, the correcting and guiding light of the Word of the living God. The work of the Christian preacher is that of relating all human action, in whatever realm, to the Divine purpose and enterprise, in order that it may be true, and strong, and lasting.

It follows that a man called to be the instrument of such service must himself live in the spiritual atmosphere. This means that he must practise the presence of God. This is much more than accepting the theory of the Divine immanence. It is the persistent and perpetual relating of all personal thought and action to that Presence. This demands, first of all, the exercise of the spiritual faculties. Inquiry must be made of God, as to what the way and the will of God may be, with regard to everything, the great and the small, the small as earnestly as the great. Not only must there be inquiry, the spirit must be trained to wait and to listen. The haste that cannot wait on the Lord must be denied. If there is not time to seek the Lord, there is not time to do anything. The doing that begins without the discovery of the Divine will is indeed deadly. All this in turn calls for response to the demands which are made as the result of such inquiry and such waiting. There must be the yielding of the judgment, that is the renewing of the mind; the consent of the heart, that is the dedication of the affection; and implicit obedience, that is the yielding of the will. This life, actively in the spiritual world, must be resolute, and continuous. No man can fulfil his ministry in spiritual things, save as he himself is living in right relation with spiritual things. When the Word ceases to be a light, a fire, a joy to a man in his own life, searching, energizing, heartening him; his preaching of it becomes a weariness, a drudgery to his own soul, and utterly ineffective in the lives of others.

Of true spiritual life for the minister of the Word, as for all others, there is a twofold condition, and test, in the realm of the material. No divorce between the body and the spirit is possible in this life. The body is the instrument of the spirit. No separation between ordinary human affairs, and the things of the spirit, is possible in this world. The things of everyday life are the opportunities of spiritual realization and expression. The condition for true personal spirituality is bodily fitness. The test of spirituality is the use a man makes of his body. Not by its destruction does he demonstrate his spiritual attainment, but by its possession and use. The opportunities for spiritual service are the commonplaces of everyday life. The test of spirituality is the use a man makes of these opportunities. Not by escape from them does he demonstrate his spirituality, but by their sanctification and beautifying. To minister the

Word so as to produce these results in the lives of others must be to live by the Word in this very sense. No minister of the Word can neglect the habits of the spiritual life without disaster to his own soul, and to his work therefore.

The second matter of importance is that of the persistent study of the Word on the part of the minister. This seems so obvious as to need no argument, and yet I fear that it is at this point that very many have sadly failed. In the years of preparation much has been done, in the very necessity of the case; and all that has been done is of the greatest value. Indeed the real value of the technical work of these years will only now begin to be known. Nevertheless all this has been preparatory. By that I do not mean preparatory to preaching merely, though of course that is true. I mean preparatory to that particular study of the Word which must be undertaken, as the definite work of the ministry is taken up. The minister will now turn to the Word in the company of his work, as he goes to his work in the company of the Word. That is to say, he will not now go to his Bible in order to discover its teaching in the abstract merely. He will turn to it, burdened with the needs, the problems, yes, and the agonies of men; in order to seek its light upon these things, so that his ministry may be a service of direction, of healing, of help. To sit down in happy seclusion, separated from all men and matters, in order to know the Scriptures, is one thing, and a great and joyful thing. It is quite another matter to go into seclusion, carrying in with you the sins and sorrows of human souls in order to find the Divine salvation and comfort. Happy indeed is the man who has had a thorough training in the former method. That will be of inestimable value now. But he cannot wholly depend on it. He must go back to a yet more diligent devotion to study. Using our great phrase, " The Word of God," as referring to the Sacred Writings, I declare that its deepest tones are never heard, its most wonderful revelation is never known, until great human need appeals to it. The minister of the Word must make that appeal vicariously, for those to whom he is called upon to minister.

Who that has been long in the work has not known the travail and the triumph of this experience? It is an awful and a glorious thing to be made the bearer of the sin, the shame, the suffering of human souls; to carry these things into the light of the Divine revelation; to hear its message of power, of hope, of comfort; and then to minister to those in need. The man who does not so continue to be a student of the Word will fail in the exercise of his ministry, however talented he may be in other ways.

Here then is a peril which confronts a man as he leaves his college and commences his work. We are apt to think that in the days of preparation we have done our work, and that we know our Bibles. We are tempted to turn to human opinions, even to be enamoured of that illusory, ephemeral, anæmic thing called "current thought." Let us guard against the temptation from the very beginning, and continuously. In the comparatively small compass of our Bibles we shall find all that the human soul needs. While we may have much help from other literature in illustration and interpretation, let us never forget that of all other writings in comparison with the Bible it may be said,

"These are but broken lights of Thee."

Therefore let us be diligent students of the Word.

It is not the purpose of these lectures to give

anything like technical details, but I may at least give a general suggestion as to a minister's method. First, let his library be carefully chosen, and let it be good, rather than large. To any man beginning the work of library building I should say, let these words guide you, *Exegesis, Exposition, Everything.* Keep that order. Never make the worst blunder of all, that of getting *everything* first. Neither make perhaps the more common mistake of putting *exposition* in the place of *exegesis.* The former is at best very often no more than the opinions of others. The latter will, in the proportion in which it is really scholarly, help you to know what the Word really says.

Then I would urge every minister as he commences his actual work to get a new Bible, and begin all over again, giving special attention to two matters. First, let him turn to the books he thinks he knows best, in order to find how much there is that he had not discovered. Then let him resolutely turn to the parts least known, most neglected, determined to face and to know them. As I have said before, for my illustrations I apologize, but not for my contention. No man can be a successful minister of the Word—and I use the word successful in its best sense—who ceases to be a student of the Word. Let me add that no man need fear that he will exhaust its treasures.

The third matter of importance is that of purposeful preaching. All preaching, whether apostolic, prophetic, evangelistic, or pastoral, has one aim; that namely of the capture of the central citadel of Mansoul, the will. The intellect and the emotions are highways of approach, and both should be employed. The one thing of which we need to be constantly reminding ourselves, is that we have never accomplished the real end of preaching until we have reached the will, and constrained it towards the choices which are in harmony with the Truth which we declare. I say "*constrained it*" towards these choices, rather than "*compelled it*" to them, for this latter we can never do. The former we may, and it is our one business to do so. To instruct the intelligence is necessary, but it is a means to an end, rather than an end. The last word of the preacher along these lines is, "If ye know these things, happy are ye if ye do them." It is in order to the doing of the will of God that His will is to be made known. To touch and move the emotions is perfectly proper, but it also is a means to an end, rather than an end. The last word of the preacher along these lines must ever be that of the Lord, " If ye love Me ye will keep My commandments." That man is indeed happy, who, himself instructed in the things of God, and inspired by the love of God, can storm the citadel of human will, along the avenues of intelligence and emotion, capturing it for his Lord, and constraining it to obedience to His Word.

The minister of the Word has two questions which he must always ask himself concerning his preaching; first, What is the need I am to address? Secondly, What is the message I am to deliver? The answer to the first is known fundamentally and essentially. He always speaks to the deepest things in human life, the things of the spirit, the things that are of abiding importance, and which touch and influence finally all the secondary things. But these things have an almost infinite variety of incidental expression; and the man who would preach the Word prevailingly to his fellow men must live among them; he must know the human spirit as well as the Word of God. His business must be to know the need he addresses.

Knowing this need he must then seek his

message. Here again inclusively he is never at a loss. That by which man lives, in the deepest of his life, is the Word of God. But the incidental application must be as varied as is the incidental expression; and he who would preach the Word prevailingly must live with the Word; he must know the Word of God as well as the human spirit. His business must be to know the remedy for the need he addresses.

Besides these two, no other question is really important. The preacher is not to ask whether they will hear or whether they will forbear; although the passion of his soul must be to persuade them to obey. He will never halt in the delivery of his message to inquire as to whether it is likely to be pleasant or disturbing. Neither of these is necessarily authoritative, and this the preacher should remember. To some temperaments there is always the temptation to think that the unpleasant is the true and the powerful. Others are tempted to imagine that the restful is the only valuable note. Both ideas are equally false. The Word of God will sometimes shake the very foundations, and disturb the spirit to its depths; while at others it will come as peace and quietness, calming all the storm into rest. The passing effects of the

Word are nothing. The ultimate victory in the sanctification of men and women to the will of God is everything.

The preacher therefore has always two supreme duties in preaching, beyond the proclamation of his message. They are those of application and appeal. The Word declared must be applied to the need as it is known. This must be done with knowledge and discretion; but it must be done, or the preaching may fail to realize its highest intention and purpose. Moreover he must appeal to the will, calling it to surrender in the name of the Lord. This appeal must be made with conviction as well as with passion. Passion characterized by unreality is of no avail; it is worse than conviction without passion. Painted fire never burns. But conviction without passion often fails to reach its goal. Unlit fuel never burns.

Let ministers of the Word preach the things of which they themselves know the power, and preach them with the passionate earnestness of which such things are worthy, and the ministry will be a constant triumph and a perpetual joy; even if it be also a constant travail, and perpetual fellowship with the sufferings of the Lord.

The final matter in the exercise of vocation is that of the patient shepherding of those who are gathered into the flock as the result of preaching. The word shepherding has application principally to the distinctly pastoral office, but the principles involved apply in each case. In apostolic ministry there is need for such detailed interpretation as may be necessary to meet the need of individual cases. In prophetic ministry, administration as well as application will constantly be called for. In evangelistic ministry, personal direction will inevitably be necessary. In each case much more than surface knowledge is demanded, both of the message and of the men to be instructed, guided, directed.

I propose to confine myself to the more strictly pastoral phase. Here there must first be the perpetual feeding of the flock by the systematic teaching of the Word. The work of the Pastor in this regard is not completely done by preaching from isolated texts. It goes without saying that it is not done at all by preaching about topics, save as they are dealt with in the light of the Word. It is the business of the Pastor and Teacher to lead the people under his care in careful and intelligent study of the Sacred Writings. Every Church should be a Bible School, a Bible College, and its minister should take oversight of all Biblical teaching, from the Primary Department of his Sunday School, through every grade, and up to the oldest members of the Church. Much of the detail work he must delegate to others, but nothing of it should be outside his knowledge and direction. His charge is to feed the lambs, and the sheep.

I refrain from discussion of methods in detail, contenting myself with this statement of a broad principle, which I hold to be of great importance.

Beyond this, however, the Pastor has a double duty. He must take oversight of the flock, and he must guide it. What John Ruskin said of the Bishops in *Sesame and Lilies* is true of all shepherds of the flock. If they do not know their people and their needs they are no bishops. Here is the true place of pastoral visitation. This however is a whole subject, and in some senses a separate one. I refer to it because it ought to have the closest relation to the ministry of the Word. It is by this method that the true Pastor discovers the needs of his people, and so knows how to bring forth things new and old out of his treasury. It goes without saying that pastoral visitation is much more than calling at houses, drinking tea, and indulging in profitless conversation.

His guidance of his flock is a sacred duty, also. Sometimes it is his duty to indicate a worthy line of conduct, even when his advice is not sought. This is not always easy; it is at times found to be unwelcome, even resented; but if he is faithful to his duty it must be done, and it is wonderful how responsive the human soul is to such guidance. Such guidance is constantly sought, and the methods of private personal interviews and correspondence are of great value in shepherding the sheep.

There is yet another thing the Pastor may have to do. He may have to fight. There are still evil, wolfish interests, and human beings who prowl around the flock to destroy, and with such the shepherd is always at war.

In view of all these responsibilities,—which are privileges also because they are shared with the Good, the Great, the Chief Shepherd,—how important it ever is that the Pastor should define his spiritual relationship with his people clearly. He should see to it that he establish no relation with them, either political or social, which would prevent his fulfilment in their lives of his high spiritual function.

To realize this ideal of the exercise of the vocation of the ministry of the Word will give the minister no spare time. It will, however, demand recreative intervals, in which, escaping entirely from all the particular work of his sacred office, he finds renewal and recuperation. Such intervals should be marked off as sacred, and no pressure of work should be allowed to interfere. To say that is to have to add; "Lord, have mercy upon us, miserable offenders, and incline our hearts to keep this law."

But again this conception as the goal of endeavour will preserve the minister from any sense of failing interest. It will often almost burden him that his opportunities are so vast, never that they are narrow. With every passing year, the Word to which he yields himself that he may give it to others, will grow in strength and beauty, and the joy of declaring it will be his strength as well as his duty.

EPILOGUE

IN our introductory study we considered the setting of the phrase which has constituted our Theme. In conclusion we return to that setting. In the statement of which the phrase is a part, we find two activities referred to, both of which are qualified by an attitude of mind, and a corresponding output of energy; "We will continue stedfastly in prayer, and in the ministry of the Word." The activities are those of "prayer" and "the ministry of the Word"; the attitude is that of "continuing stedfastly."

The attitude indicated was that of the whole Church. In the strangely mysterious days between the ascension and Pentecost, they "*continued stedfastly* in prayer." After Pentecost the Apostles and early disciples, together with those brought into the company through Peter's preaching, "*continued stedfastly* in the Apostles' teaching, and fellowship; in the breaking of bread, and the prayers."

Now in the case of the Twelve the attitude

had special application to two matters,
" Prayer," and " The Ministry of the Word."
This meant limitation; but such limitation as
made for intensity in the direction indicated;
and so limitation, in the interest of the whole
fellowship of the Church, and of its mission in
the world. All the other duties of the Fellowship were most sacred, but they were to be at-
tended to by others. These men, in the spirit
of continuing stedfastness, which was the spirit
of all, were to do two things; they were to
pray; and they were to serve the Word.

Having completed our consideration of the
ministry of the Word, we pause in conclusion
to remember the work which is first named,
that of Prayer. This work is thus first named,
because it is preliminary; and it is connected,
because it must be continuous. Nothing more
is necessary in this connection than a most
simple examination of the idea of continuing
stedfastly in prayer.

The word for prayer in this passage is at once
the most common in use, and the most inclusive
in suggestion. It is the word *prŏsĕuchŏmai*, a
compound word, made up of the preposition
prŏs, and the verb *ĕuchŏmai*. The preposition
suggests motion towards a goal; while the verb

simply means to wish, to desire. The simplest idea then of prayer is that of desire towards God. The word is always used of prayer to the gods or to God. It includes the whole attitude and activities of prostration in worship, of the sense of dependence, and of the expression of desire.

The phrase "continued stedfastly" is the translation of one Greek word *prŏskartĕrĕō*, which again is a compound of the same preposition *prŏs*, and the verb *kartĕrĕō*, which means to be strong; that is, earnest, determined in effort. Thus the whole word indicates persistent, powerful perseverance.

It is thus that those called to the ministry of the Word are to pray. The prayer attitude is that of a consciousness of need, of dependence upon God; and of perfect confidence in God. Apart from this attitude and activity, no man can fulfil his ministry of the Word. The question, "Who is sufficient for these things?" and the answer, "Our sufficiency is of God," combine to inspire earnest and persistent prayer, in the power of which the ministry of the Word may be exercised.

It is then of the utmost importance that, from the first, the man called to this ministry should cultivate the habits of prayer. This needs to be done. The habits of the religious life are no more spontaneous than are those of the godless life. It is by the doing of things regularly, systematically, and of set purpose, that the time comes when they are done habitually.

The habits of prayer are of two kinds; which may be described as the regular and the irregular. The regular habits are those of set times and places and forms. These should be arranged according to temperament and opportunity, and then rigidly adhered to. The minister's study should be first of all his oratory; the place into which he can go and shut the door against all intruders; and that not only, and not first, to study, but to pray.

The irregular habits of prayer are those in which the soul is trained to the perpetually Godward attitude in thought, in purpose, in activity. Thus prayer will be ejaculatory, or unuttered as to words even in thought; the Godward desire perpetually operating, and so influencing all thinking, all loving, all doing. Than this, nothing is more important, or more potential. It is thus that we may pray without ceasing.

To continue stedfastly in preaching, it is necessary to do so in prayer. There must be
prayer in preparation, for the shining of the
true light upon the holy page, for the interpretation of the One Interpreter. There must be
prayer in preaching, for the coöperation of that
Spirit, through Whom the demonstration, or
making plain, alone can come to the hearers.
There must be prayer in all the pastoral work
which follows preaching, for true wisdom in
dealing with those who are to be, not only instructed in the Truth, but led into obedience to
its claims in all manner of behaviour. Granted
the man gifted, trained, and continuing stedfastly in prayer, the ministry of the Word
through him will be powerful and prevailing.

This is to dismiss a subject of overwhelming
importance with almost discourteous brevity.
It is so dismissed, not from lack of the sense of
urgency, but on account of the limitations of
my present theme. Under other conditions
there is nothing I should count a greater privilege than to speak at length on the vital relation
between prayer and preaching. Here and now
I must content myself with this brief and con-
densed reference to that relationship. If there
is one thing of which experience has made me

more sure than of anything else, it is that there can be no fruitful and victorious ministry of the Word, which is not conditioned from first to last, not only in the sense of dependence upon God, but also in the active expression of it, which has been made available to us in the sacred privilege of prayer.

The briefest backward glance over the ground we have traversed will illustrate and emphasize this matter. Service, or Ministry, can only be intelligently rendered as the servants or ministers of the Word hold constant converse with Him of Whom the Word is the Expression, through the Word Who is His perfect exegesis. The Word can only be rightly apprehended as the interpretation of the Spirit is sought, and that persistently. The Apostle who is to render it available to men by translation or systematization needs all the time to ask for guidance. The Prophet proclaiming it to his age needs to remember that it only becomes potential as it is delivered in the power of the Spirit, and accompanied in the delivery by His demonstration; and for this coöperation he must ever seek in prayer. The Evangelist can only combine the warning and wooing notes in the harmony of his message, as in

prayer he gains that preparation of spirit necessary to so delicate and glorious a task. The
Pastor and Teacher will be perpetually driven
by the very variety of the claims made upon
him, to seek in the Secret Place the direction of
the One Great Shepherd of the flock.

To meet the changed conditions of to-day in
loyalty to the unchanged obligations of his ministry, every preacher will need to guard his own
mind and heart and will by diligent cultivation
of communion with God in prayer. Through
all the perilous processes of training, men need
prayer, prayer, and always prayer. When we
pass out from training to the exercise of the
holy vocation, then perhaps it is more true of
us than of any man, and more true than at any
time, that " men ought always to pray, and not
to faint."

Perhaps the final word on this matter, to be
spoken with reverent reticence, and yet to be
uttered unhesitatingly, is that The Word of
God, in days of limitation, resulting from His
infinite Self-emptying, found necessary the long
quiet seasons of communion with God alone
upon the mountains; and constantly interrupted
even His public speech, to offer praise or prayer
to His Father.

Surely then for us in the Ministry of the Word, the final injunction, exhortation, should be, Let us pray, and that without ceasing.

Printed in the United States of America

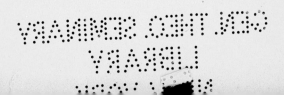